SAINT BENEDICT

A Rule for Beginners

D1288587

SAINT BENEDICT

A Rule for Beginners

Excerpts from the Life and Rule of Saint Benedict
edited with an introduction and commentary

by

Julian Stead, O.S.B.

preface by
Benedict J. Groeschel, C.F.R.

New City Press

Published in the United States by New City Press
202 Cardinal Rd., Hyde Park, NY 12538
©1994 New City Press

Cover picture: Saint Benedict, Conxolus, thirteenth century, Subiaco, Sacro Speco. Used with permission.

Library of Congress Cataloging-in-Publication Data:

Stead, Julian.
    Saint Benedict : a rule for beginners / Julian Stead.

    Includes bibliographical references.
    ISBN 1-56548-098-8
    1. Benedict, Saint, Abbot of Monte Cassino.   2. Benedict, Saint,
Abbot of Monte Cassino, Regula.   3. Gregory I, Pope, ca. 540-604.
De vita et miraculis venerabilis Benedicti.   4. Benedictines—Rule.
5. Benedictines—Spiritual life.   6. Monastic and religious life.
7. Spiritual life—Catholic Church.   8. Catholic Church—Doctrines.
I. Title.
BR1720.B45S74   1993
255'.106—dc20   93-2544

1st printing: October 1993
5th printing: January 2002

Printed in Canada

Contents

Preface

It was only a few decades ago that students of Church history or of apologetics paused to give an admiring nod to Saint Benedict and the monks of the West for saving civilization during the Dark Ages, the five or six centuries extending from the collapse of the Roman Empire to the bright dawn of medieval culture in the twelfth century. But in those days of strong religious identity we did not spend much time on the Dark Ages, because we were busy gathering in the harvest that had been planted in the Catholic reformation and in the surprising spiritual revival that marked the end of the nineteenth century and carried on until after the Second World War. Who needed the Dark Ages, especially in the bright days of Vatican II? The world was about to accept the Church with open arms—or so we thought. The only real obstacle was the Communist tyranny in much of the world, but many suspected that it would either fall apart, evolve into something better, or even be converted. With technology and the irresistible spread of democracy the Church would be part of an ever improving humanity and on an ever more intelligently utilized planet.

However, less than three decades later many thoughtful people are wondering if we are on the threshold of a second Dark Ages, and some even more thoughtful people are trying to discern how we can survive the collapsing foundations of western civilization and even the decline of all humanizing culture. Communism is gone, and its demise did not usher in the millennium. Religious indifference vies with religious ignorance to produce a very dark picture inside the Church itself. One cannot seriously ponder the present scene without recalling two great thinkers from the past: Saint Augustine and Saint Benedict. Augustine led the Fathers of the Church in providing a light to shine through the Dark Ages, summing up as he did the impact of the gospel on the Greco Roman civilization. Augustine, especially in the West, was the great mind that reflected the impact of divine revelation in the person of Christ on the classical tradition. But a light is useless unless it has a lamp to sustain it and this became Saint Benedict's role.

As Julian Stead, O.S.B. makes clear, Benedict was not a speculative thinker, a philosopher-theologian. He was a very practical spiritual father,

7

who worked in a down to earth way to help his fellow Christians find their way back to their heavenly homeland. This beautiful summary of Benedict's teaching is by a man who has faithfully lived the Benedictine life for more than half a century. It is a valuable and clear presentation of the spirit of that one who provided the lamps and kept them burning throughout the Dark Ages, and in many cases since then.

Although Augustine must be counted along with the other founders of religious life in the West, the task of spreading Christian community life fell to the monks of Saint Benedict. Without in any way implying a criticism of the Augustinian religious in the Dark Ages, all will agree that it was the followers of the Rule of Saint Benedict who were the most numerous and their impact more widespread. It was the sons of Saint Benedict who not only brought the scriptures but also the works of the Fathers and the elements of civilization to the dark forests of the North. It was largely in Benedictine abbeys that Christianity and culture was kept alive.

If one admits that this time of ours has similarities to those dark times and especially has echoes of the end of the empire, then Saint Benedict may well be seen as having more and more to say to us. My own contacts with Benedictine monks and nuns, as well as with lay oblates, have convinced me that not only does the father of the western monasticism have a contribution to make now, but he can provide guidance for sincere Christians whatever their specific spirituality may be. To use a phrase borrowed from the historian Barbara Tuchman, Benedict holds a distant mirror to our own time.

Father Julian has carefully selected several substantial elements of the Benedictine corpus of writings and has commented on these with wisdom and wit. Each chapter stands by itself and presents another aspect of the saint's thought. I found the chapter on God most intriguing and the chapters on humility painfully enlightening. When the thought of any g. eat saint such as Augustine, Benedict or Francis is taken out of the past, it is necessary to relate their insights to our own times; otherwise they are simply like pictures in a book. The more ancient the writer, the more obvious is the need. Father Julian fulfills this need very well. The distilled ideas, adjustments and insights of a life of Benedictine discipleship are in evidence in this book. The readers will feel that they are receiving the same hospitality that Saint Benedict emphatically required of his monks and his sister Saint Scholastica enjoined on the nuns. As one who has often gratefully benefitted by this hospitality in monasteries as far removed as Montserrat and Boulder, Colorado, I can only heartily encourage the reader to pursue the following pages gracefully, prayerfully and slowly. The distressing scene around us in Church and state may indeed remind us of a dark age, but then this book recalls that even in such times there were places of refreshment, light, peace and discipleship. Perhaps because we are living in days similar to the ones that Ferdinand Lott described so well in his study *The End of the Roman Empire and the Beginning of the Dark Ages*, we might do well to ponder his observations on what saved civilization. He reminds us that it was the monasteries that shone like islands of light in a dark sea of barbarism and provided the only refuge for a sensitive and cultured person. Anyone interested in Christian culture or, in fact, in civilization of any kind, can only value and profit from the spirit of Saint Benedict, so beautifully captured in this work of loving dedication.

Benedict J. Groeschel, C.F.R.

Introduction

There are already enough editions, translations, and commentaries on the Rule of Saint Benedict to fill a fair-sized library. Why offer another? Because it is such a phenomenal gold mine of practical wisdom and of understanding of human nature, not only of its problems and how to overcome them, but also of our potential for goodness and how to fulfill it. We are offering here selections from *Saint Benedict's Rule for Monasteries* and from the *Life and Miracles of Saint Benedict*, with some commentary, relevant to people aspiring to a better life at the turn of the twenty-first century.

Where did Benedict acquire this wisdom? Augustine Baker (a Welshman who lived in Elizabethan England and became a Benedictine, first in Padua, Italy) thought Benedict's only teacher was the Holy Spirit. But this is an over-simplification. Modern research shows him to have been well read in scripture and some of the Fathers. From the Old Testament he quotes predominantly from the psalms and the sapiential books: Proverbs, Wisdom, and Sirach; from the New Testament: the Gospels according to Matthew and Luke, the Letters of Paul, and the First Letter of Peter (there are *many* similarities between the latter and Saint Benedict's Rule). But an equal number of his words have been shown to be derived from Christian writers who preceded him by a century or more.

He was concerned with life, not speculation. He says in the final chapter of the Rule that he wrote it to help people achieve at least some measure of wholesome goodness together, while they hasten to their heavenly home. Just "a little Rule for beginners." Go to the saints, he says, if you want to achieve the heights of sanctity. "For him who would hasten to the perfection of that life, there are the teachings of the holy Catholic Fathers, by observing which a person is led to the summits of perfection. . . . What book [of theirs] does not loudly proclaim how we may come by a straight course to our Creator?"

There is no indication that he grappled with proofs of the existence of God, the mysteries of the mutual relations of the three Divine Persons and of divinity and humanity within Christ; nor with the proofs of the divine origin of the Church and her defense against critics, which exercised the genius of so many saints in the Church's first seven centuries.[1] He does not draw much from, or comment on, the gospel of John and the more speculative heights of Paul's letters, nor the Book of Revelation. In the writings of the Fathers, it is the lives and moral teachings of the saints that he recommends to our reading, and that presumably he found inspirational for himself. From the great Doctors of the Church, Augustine for instance, it is mostly from his *letters* that he quotes, and from Basil's monastic Rule. Jerome (340-420 A.D.) was a practical soul; in that respect, and in his love of Christ, he was a kindred spirit to Benedict, who however did not engage in the kind of rhetoric and satire of which Jerome was fond; Benedict excised satirical passages, for instance, when quoting from the Rule of the Master. Benedict discourages laughter.

The Rule of the Master was a monastic rule written at about the same time as the Rule of Benedict but three times as long. There is now no reasonable doubt that Benedict's Rule is a digest of it, although up until the twentieth century it was thought that the Master came later. Benedict's gentleness is reflected in what he left out or modified.

Leaders in the religious world—or professionals, if you like—have to avoid two extremes: fanaticism and mediocrity. No one knows who the Master was (an unlikely theory is that he was Benedict himself, who mellowed in his more advanced age), but the Master certainly falls into the category of fanatics. What label to put on the mean between the extremes is not easy to choose. "Enthusiasm" might do, but enthusiasm can be purely emotional and can cross the border into fanaticism.

In one of those last six chapters of his Rule which are Benedict's own and bear no dependency on the Master, he calls this balanced virtue "Good Zeal." It is worth quoting in its entirety: "Just as there is an evil zeal of bitterness which separates from God and leads to hell, so there is a good zeal which separates from vices and leads to God and life everlasting. This zeal therefore the monks should practice with the most fervent love. Let them, that is, 'in honor prefer one another' (Rom 12:10). Let them bear with the greatest patience one another's infirmities, whether of body or character. Let them vie in paying obedience to one another. Let none follow what seems good for himself but rather what is good for another. Tender the charity of brotherhood chastely. Let them fear God in love and love their abbot with a

---

1. He lived in the fifth and sixth, probable dates: 480-545.

sincere and humble charity. Let them prefer nothing whatever to Christ; and may he bring us all alike to life everlasting" (*Rule* 72).

Speaking from experience, Benedict was aware that there is a real danger of *bitterness* in religious life: the bitterness of disillusion—which T.S. Eliot has said is the final illusion. A man might have come to the monastery expecting to experience enlightenment, only to find inner darkness. The illusion consisted in not recognizing that the darkness *is* enlightenment: the enlightenment of realizing that the ultimately desirable truths lie above and beyond our narrow mind's comprehension. Some monks fail to enjoy the contemplation of mystery, fail to adore the incomprehensible, are too proud to be content with not knowing all the answers.

Another is bitter because monastic life is not quite what he expected; work he enjoyed has been given to someone else, who does it differently; the abbot or his brothers do not follow his advice; changes have been adopted, or those he expected to occur have not materialized. Some monks do not seem to like him very much, or he does not like the younger ones who show him no special deference. He regrets leaving his family and the affection he imagines he would have enjoyed from a wife and children. He misses home. It is the age-old problem of "the far hills are green," or "the grass on the other side of the fence is greener."

Again another monk, Benedict might well have seen, grows bitterly disillusioned because his brothers in the monastery are just like ordinary people. Some keep him awake by snoring or coughing all night. Perhaps he is made to take care of a more or less senile old monk; a stroke victim can lose control of his bodily or mental functions and be very trying. A monk with good zeal will bear their infirmities whether of body or character with the greatest patience, even with joy. We do not know how much their education in his time resembled the kind of education given in convent or monastery schools today, but Benedict presupposes there will be boys (or in convents, girls) entrusted to the care of the community. "Everywhere let them have supervision and discipline," he writes, "until they come to the age of discretion." "Boys are to be kept under discipline at all times and by everyone. The juniors shall honor their seniors, and the seniors love their juniors." "As often as faults are committed by boys, or by youths . . . let such offenders be punished with severe fasts or chastised with sharp stripes, in order that they may be cured" (*Rule* 63 and 30). Times change; far from being required to fast, students in Benedictine schools today may be punished by

being required to come to an otherwise optional early breakfast before going
to classes, instead of exercising the privilege to sleep late. (And corporal
punishment is out.) The means are adapted to times and circumstances, but
the need and the purpose of curing weaknesses remains always the same.
Taking care of children, or adolescents, or the elderly can take a great deal
of patience and tolerance, and the monk can grow tired of it and grow bitterly
aware that he has no more peace here than he might have had in a family of
his own. But here he has not the stimulus of natural affection for his own
children and old mom or dad. The trials of family life are not to be expected
to be missing in a Benedictine house. Why should they be? And the values
Benedict sees in community life can also be found in the life of a Christian
family.

Benedict devotes a whole chapter of his Rule to the "Care of Old Men
and Children": "Although human nature itself is drawn to pity toward these
times of life . . . yet let them be provided for by the authority of the Rule. Let
there be constant consideration for their weakness, and on no account let the
rigor of the Rule be applied to them. Let them, on the contrary, receive
compassionate consideration" (*Rule* 37). And regarding the sick: "Before all
things and above all things care must be taken of the sick, so that they may
be served as Christ himself; for he said: 'I was sick and you visited me'; and,
'what you did to one of these least ones, you did unto me.' But let the sick
on their part consider that they are being served for the honor of God and not
provoke their brothers who are serving them by unreasonable demands. Yet
they should be patiently borne with, because from such as these is gained a
more abundant reward" (*Rule* 36). To urge his monks to serve the young, the
sick, and the old with "good zeal," though one does not feel the natural
affection felt for one's own flesh and blood, he reminds them "to fear and
love God," "to prefer nothing to Christ," whom they are to see in their weaker
brothers. Only this love of Christ can motivate their zeal and make them go
beyond natural affection.

The words in Benedict's Rule are carefully chosen, and we have not said
much about "bearing with the greatest patience one another's infirmities of
. . . *character*" (in Latin, *mores*, which means customs, manners, and
morals). If a man wanted to join his community, Benedict would accept him
if he would put up with being kept waiting outside four or five days, and
another few days in the guest house.

All who came as guests for a few days were "to be received like Christ,

for he will say: 'I was a stranger and you took me in' (Mt 25:35)," at any
hour of the day. "Special attention should be shown to the poor and to
pilgrims, because in them Christ is more truly welcomed" (*Rule* 53). So that
the brothers would not be disturbed by the arrival of guests at irregular hours,
there were separate dining quarters "for the abbot and guests." So the abbot
himself ate with the guests, apart from his monks, perhaps to show them
honor (Christ was received in them), perhaps as a sort of apostolate without
going out of his monastery grounds, perhaps to judge the suitability and
motives of any who were hoping to be received as novices into the monastery.
The novices also ate and slept apart from the "professed" monks.

But reading between the lines, as well as what we know from historical
sources, Benedict's monastery must have been quite an assortment, in terms
of the monks' racial, social, and cultural background. Some, like Benedict
himself, were from Roman families, something like "Southern gentlemen";
others were illiterates belonging to the invading tribes; others would be native
peasants, some of whom might have been illiterate. There were no require-
ments such as in many monasteries today of a high school diploma or even
a college degree. (According to his biographer, Benedict himself was a
college drop-out.) Neither Benedict himself nor his monks were priests;
"abbot" did not connote what it means today, a prelate in the Church. He was
simply a layman with charisma for teaching others the spiritual life, analogous to the head coach of a football team, a ship's captain, the top administrator of a hospital or high school, running a "school of the Lord's way of
service"; Benedict also likens him to a "physician . . . who has undertaken
the charge of weakly souls."

Patience with these "weakly souls" could test the zeal of anyone; they
would be bitterly disappointed if they entered a monastery and expected it to
be inhabited by nothing but angels. When his novitiate was over, at the end
of one year, a new monk was dressed in the clothes of the monastery, and
turned in his former clothes to symbolize what Paul called "putting off the
old self" (Adam) and clothing himself with "the new self" (Christ). But the
Adam in us does not automatically die, just by our moving into a new place
and putting on a new set of clothes to symbolize the starting of a new life; he
goes down fighting. The new self gradually—if ever at all—consumes and
digests into himself the old self hidden beneath the monastic uniform (or
"habit"). The customs, manners, and morals of the old self include idiosyncracies and weaknesses, even perversity, which can be hard to bear with.

Only the monk who zealously sees the face of Christ in his brothers can find God in them and in associating with them. Otherwise he may find himself bitterly disappointed and become separated from God. He may think it is on their account, but the fault is his more than theirs: a lack of humility about himself and a lack of faith about the presence of Christ in these "least ones," who are the very type Christ came to serve and save.

Much of the Rule contains warnings against what can go wrong in monastic life. Reading between the lines, a historical novel could be written depicting what real life was probably like in Benedict's own monastery; all the challenges, frustrations, and disappointments he must have faced as a shepherd and physician of souls might make amusing or depressing reading, depending on the novelist's style and the expectations of the reader. Clearly he did not have to deal with ready-made saints. He suffered plenty from the men he tried to serve. In his Prologue he warns his disciples that they may easily become discouraged and give up, because the beginnings of the spiritual life "cannot but be narrow" (*angustus*, the Latin word for narrow, is the root of our word "anguish"). We have to wade against the current of the world around us and of fallen nature within us. "The amendment of vices or the preservation of charity" calls for "a certain strictness," but Benedict hopes it will not be found "harsh or burdensome." He is assuming that vices will crop up and charity will at least be threatened; it is a rough and narrow road in the beginning, but he urges us to keep trying, promising that "as we advance in the religious life and in faith, our hearts expand and we run the way of God's commandments with unspeakable sweetness of love." He has had experience of both the negative and the positive, of failures and successes; and he seems to know of "Murphy's Law": that if anything *can* go wrong, it will.

Little phrases keep cropping up in his Rule which betray Benedict as a man in love with Christ, not with himself, who also fears not the judgment of history but the judgment of Christ. For instance, "Let the abbot always bear in mind [always!] that at the dread Judgment of God there will be an examination of . . . his teaching and the obedience of his disciples. . . . Any lack of profit the master of the house" (who is God, or Christ dwelling invisibly in their midst—not the abbot himself) "may find in the sheep will be laid to the blame of the shepherd." (Let parents take heed.)

Because they "fear God in love," and "prefer nothing whatever to Christ," monks must "vie in paying obedience one to another," "following what benefits another" rather than oneself, "tender the charity of brotherhood chastely," and "love their abbot." He discovered that we are only loving ourselves or a figment of our imagination, if we think we love God but cannot stand the test of loving our neighbor. We are really encountering Christ when we encounter our brother or sister; living in that faith, when we give up our own will or taste or imagined good, to do the will of another or what benefits another, it is Christ's will we are doing, Christ we are pleasing or benefiting, though he may be disfigured (or "crucified" if you like) in the guise of our neighbor. Christ is encountered in the vicious and the sinful as well as in the saint: in people of every age in life, in the sick, the guests, the weak, the strong, the educated and the uneducated, as well as in the abbot.

A monk's love of God is an illusion if it does not include this kind of mutual love which Benedict terms "obedience." He has no chapter on the love of God; it is too easy to be deluded about one's love of God; what proves that it is the real thing is all the ramifications of what he calls "humility" and "obedience." Likewise, he has no chapter on "chastity," there are just little phrases like "Tender the charity of brotherhood chastely," which show how Benedict understood this indispensable Christian virtue: the right or appropriate way to love your neighbor. There is nothing wrong with friendship or affection, but it *can* go wrong, if you prefer something else to Christ.

This is why he prefers the common life to the hermit's, and why his spirituality is distinctly a community spirituality rather than an individualistic one. The love of Christ must be put to the test, or refined like precious metal, by love of neighbor. One's commitment to God's will must be proven by cooperation with the will of those who (however imperfectly) represent Christ. That is a law of the incarnation, which can also be seen as the law of the cross: of the love of God wherever he is met crucified in human weakness. At the beginning of the spiritual life people normally need a teacher and guide, as well as the support and example of others pursuing the same ideal. Strengthened by that support, having absorbed the abbot's teaching and been refined by the common life, they may then answer a call to "the solitary combat of the desert."

Benedict's Life

Benedict's life was written in the second book of the *Dialogues* of Gregory the Great (d. 604), a work which was so popular in the Middle Ages that (unusual for works by Latin Fathers) it was translated into Greek,[1] where—in the Byzantine world—Gregory is known not as "the Great" but as "the Dialoguer." This work remains enthralling to people with a taste for the preternatural, but when it is read with our scientific mentality today we cannot help wondering whether its miraculous episodes are to be considered historical or just legends. An honest, simple answer to questions about the historicity of the *Dialogues* cannot be given. The stories *could* be historically true. Or they could be historical fiction, with some basis in fact. They certainly have lessons to teach, and readers are free to judge for themselves both the value of the lessons and the reliability of the evidence for the stories' historicity. Their historical truth was never a matter of Christian *faith;* even if they were proven to be largely unhistorical, we could still find them interesting and enjoyable. No presentation of Benedict and his Rule should ignore them; they are so much a part of Benedictine tradition, indeed of the patrimony of Christian literature as a whole.

The truth is, an English scholar of impeccable credentials as a critical historian, named Francis Clark, has renewed honest doubts about Gregory's authorship of the *Dialogues*, doubts first raised by the humanists and Protestant reformers of the sixteenth century. The *Dialogues* contain excerpts or passages very similar to other works by Gregory, but Benedict does not begin to appear in the calendar of saints until a good seventy years after Gregory's death, at which time possibly another Roman composed the *Dialogues*. Be that as it may, it would be wrong to dismiss legendary or traditional histories about the saints, as if they contained no shred of truth except what can be confirmed by the modern methods of historical criticism.

For certain facts about Benedict's life there is rock-solid evidence. Excavations in the 1950's provided circumstantial evidence in support of his being born into a Roman family, leading citizens of the town of Nursia, today Norcia, in central Italy. Indeed, if we are shaped somewhat by our environment, Norcia is a likely sort of place where someone like Benedict might grow up: a self-sufficient town, still within its Roman walls, situated in the middle of a long and wide plain, fertile for agriculture, completely surrounded by mountains, not far from Assisi, where Francis was born seven hundred years later on the western slopes of the same mountains.

The tradition is that he was sent from there to Rome, much as the son of

---

1. By Pope Saint Zacharias (740-51).

the mayor of a West Virginian town might be sent to college at Georgetown. In the Trastevere region of Rome they preserve a house where he is supposed to have lived, cared for by what the British call his "nanny." Scandalized by the debauchery of the other students, he dropped out and headed for the hills beyond Tivoli, immediately to the east of Rome, still accompanied by nanny. About thirty-five miles east of the city he accepted the hospitality of a group of men trying to live the gospel devoutly together; but he created a sensation when, simply in an instant answer to his prayer, a tray which his nanny had borrowed was mended, without any trace of its former fracture. He simply could not handle all the notoriety this got him; he was not a loner, but after all he was less mature in age when he started out on his religious life than Francis, for instance, who was twenty-seven or twenty-eight when he started gathering disciples; so he stole secretly away from his nurse and with the help of a monk named Romanus found a cave to hide away in, near a lake artificially created by a Roman emperor, who had built himself a villa there. Romanus clothed him in the monastic habit and secretly kept getting food to him for three years, at the end of which time some shepherds came upon him accidentally. They recognized his holiness, broke the news, and he was soon a center of attraction. That (according to the *Dialogues*) is how he came to found, from among his visitors, the monastery of Subiaco, still flourishing. He soon built twelve monasteries along the steep slopes upstream from the lake; the only other still in use is built around his cave. They have been centers of pilgrimage ever since.

Whether or not his name was Benedict of Nursia, obviously somebody built those monasteries, and somebody wrote the Rule; the latter is not the bland kind of document that is compiled by a committee. When we see the changes or additions made to the Rule of the Master, a single clear personality emerges, and it is no wonder that people were drawn to place their lives permanently under his direction. There is no scientific evidence refuting the tradition that the founder of those monasteries was the author of the Rule.

The parish priest of Subiaco felt the crowds should be coming to him for direction rather than to this relatively uneducated lay upstart in those sylvan monasteries. A row developed, and rather than let the priest's antagonism disturb the peace—and even risk the souls—of his disciples, Benedict took a few with him and left his beloved Subiaco.

Whether or not the story of why he left Subiaco is historically verifiable, certain it is that about seventy-five miles south of Rome, on one of the main roads, lies the town of Cassino, which was defended by an ancient fortress at the summit of a 1,700 foot mountain. Within the walls of this fortress, where there were still pagan temples, Benedict established a new community. The tradition is that he was buried there, alongside his twin sister Scholastica. When the monastery was demolished from the air in World War II, the bomb which embedded itself in their tomb failed to explode. Benedict is said to have turned the temples into chapels, dedicated to Saint John the Baptist and Saint Martin (a monastic saint from fourth-century Gaul), and to have converted the locals to Christianity by his preaching. Thomas Aquinas, a Dominican, was educated in the school at Monte Cassino, seven centuries later. In 1992, another Benedictine-educated Dominican has been elected Master-General of the Order.

The life and miracles of Benedict as narrated in the *Dialogues* may be factual in each detail, but even if they are not, what we have outlined above may be considered historically certain, and the rest *at least* has didactic value, teaching values which have been respected in the Benedictine tradition. Benedict is depicted as having "the spirit of all the just," in particular of Moses, Elisha, Saint Peter, Elijah, and David; other Fathers, for example, Maximus the Confessor, a younger contemporary of Gregory, have tried to show how the ordinary Christian can be like the same and other saints. If the stories of Benedict's life attributed to Gregory are in fact fictional to a great extent, so that he appears analogous to a superman, a kind of miracle working super saint, then the author of the Rule followed the example of Mary and Joseph, who gave Christ to the world but said nothing about themselves; it was Christ's life not theirs that they wished to be known and imitated. Insofar as Benedict summed up and handed on the monastic traditions which arose, like Christianity itself, in the Middle East, under the inspiration of the Spirit of Christ, we may say he handed on the Holy Spirit as well as the incarnate Word; the gospels give Christ's teaching to his own disciples, a tiny persecuted minority; later, through the preaching of the apostles and their followers as agents of the Holy Spirit, Christ's disciples became a majority in the Roman Empire, and Christian society had to be organized; the Rules of Basil (Greek) and Pachomius (Egyptian) and the lives of the Desert Fathers were known to Benedict in Latin translation; he was not a linguist like Jerome who was bilingual in Greek and Latin and learned Hebrew so that he could make the official Latin translation of the Bible. But Benedict assimilated enough of the Eastern monastic spirit to transmit it to the West; in fact, a contemporary Benedictine scholar expressed the opinion that Benedict would be more at home in the Eastern Christian Churches today than in the Latin or Western. His Rule became the basis on which the Latin-speaking Christian society of the Middle Ages was structured, beginning in Anglo-Saxon England and spreading from there to all the countries of Europe which later became Protestant. Towns grew up around his monasteries, as betrayed sometimes in their names, like "München" or those ending in "Minster."

Benedict's Social Background

It is as difficult for us to reconstruct the social background of Benedict's life as it is to let some healthy young person feel what it is really like to suffer from severe arthritis. They were times of widespread destruction, chaos, and insecurity. Nomadic invaders were overrunning Western Europe from the East: the blue-eyed White Man and some Mongols, who could neither read nor write, and knew not the peaceful arts of agriculture, but lived by herding cattle, hunting, and also plundering the cities and towns of civilization, making even transport over the Roman system of roads risky; as a result, a couple of years of poor harvests in one province could bring starvation to the populace, neither relief nor messengers appealing for it could get through. In the face of such insecurity, the Emperor Constantine had moved the seat of government to Constantinople, nearly two centuries before Benedict's lifetime; and seventy years before his birth, the city of Rome itself finally fell to the invaders. In Benedict's own times, the great Emperor Justinian, codifier of Christian civil law, tried to re-establish Roman rule in Italy through Belisarius, one of the most brilliant military strategists of all time, but with limited success. A hundred years later things were to get worse, when Saracens began to attack Italy from the sea; in fact a town near Subiaco is inhabited by their descendants. In terms of recent history familiar to English-speaking people in the Western hemisphere, we might liken the situation to North America from the point of view of the nations which had inhabited it before the seventeenth century. But from the Roman point of view, seventh century Italy was not so bad as that; the invaders were not bent on genocide; nevertheless, scenes similar to that described at Wounded Knee in the 1860's, for which more than twenty (white) Americans were awarded the Congressional Medal of Honor, must have occurred. Italy's invaders were guilty more of vandalism, which got its name from one of the Germanic nations, than of widespread murder. They left the cities standing but considerably depopulated, with some municipal government intact, or there would have remained no Rome, Naples, or Florence. The contemporary scene might be compared to that of the Confederate States of America after they had been reconquered by the likes of Sherman, "Beast" Butler, and Sheridan. The economy was in a shambles. However, once the war between the States was over, it was over; although no Union army continued the destruction after the Southern States were restored to the Union, their culture was "gone with the wind." Western Europe, however, remained only nominally part of the Roman Empire, whose armies and civilian officials from Constantinople no longer controlled it. After three centuries, Charlemagne established a Roman Empire of the West (and imposed the Rule of Benedict on all its monasteries) with the blessing of the pope, who nevertheless kept a delegate at the court of Constantinople, which was not happy about this Frank calling himself "Roman" Emperor. The fallen structures were replaced by new ones designed by Benedict, whose concern for order and stability countered the chaos and insecurity that overwhelmed the earlier civilization of his native land.

But he could not foresee that his designs for himself and his few followers would spread all over the continent. It is a fulfillment of our Lord's parable of the mustard seed (cf. Mk 4:30-32): we never know what repercussions our words and deeds may have, long after we have ceased to be visibly present. Benedict's was a stabilizing and constructive influence. His libraries would preserve the medical science of Hippocrates and Galen, and the *Natural History* of Pliny, which would be developed by the Venerable Bede, a monk in the north of England, who was a scientist as well as a theologian, historian, and poet; Bede lived from the age of seven in his Northumbrian monastery, the center of a high (for the ancient world) civilization until it was destroyed by Danes.

Benedict believed in the value of manual labor to make the monasteries self-supporting. The barbarians learned agriculture from the monks. In fact it was monks who brought sheep-farming into medieval England and taught the populace weaving, the wool trade becoming the foundation of the national economy.

He could not have foreseen the clericalization of his monks by Gregory the Great, who sent the monks he had lived with under Benedict's Rule in Rome as missionaries to the Angles. The abbots of the monasteries established there would be royal councillors; quite late in the Middle Ages the English parliament met in the chapter house of Westminster Abbey. Benedict could not have foreseen an abbot as an *ex officio* member of the House of

Lords; it is hard to believe he would have been comfortable with the idea. As Abbot of Glastonbury (a monastery in the west of Britain which actually preceded Benedict but adopted his Rule), Saint Dunstan had educated King Edgar, who appointed him Archbishop of Canterbury—whose founding Archbishop was the Benedictine Augustine, sent by Gregory from Rome. Where else could the kings of the barbarous, war-mongering settlers in Western Europe find educated, Christian counselors and potential bishops but in the monasteries? They did not necessarily fulfill Benedict's qualifications for a suitable abbot less well because of their involvement in national affairs; some became saints.

Benedict was inspired to find a practical means to bring the order and stability of the gospel into all that chaos and insecurity. But such a political economy and society would not be viable in the physical world, unless first the people who implemented it were converted spiritually. His spirituality (which was not "his" but Christ's) had "to root up and tear down, to destroy and demolish" the residue of original sin, in order "to build and to plant" the reign of God (cf. Jer 2:10).

What Benedict built and planted never completely collapsed or died, but his monasteries lost their virtual monopoly of religious life in the Catholic Church with the rise of centralized religious orders, better able to respond to new situations. The monasteries had been lighthouses on islands in a dark sea. Feudalism gave way to urban capitalism, heresies were appearing or reappearing, pre-Christian philosophy infiltrated newly established universities. The Benedictines did not resist the emergence of the religious orders; in one way or another they supported and contributed to them. As my novice master used to say, "Benedictines are Catholics"; we willingly learn from new movements in the Church, much as Benedict suggests we may do from the Fathers: "For him who would hasten to perfection there are the teachings of the holy Fathers. . . . What else are they but tools of virtue for right-living and obedient monks? But for us who are lazy and ill-living and negligent they are a source of shame and confusion.

"Whoever you are, therefore, who are hastening to the heavenly homeland, fulfill with the help of Christ this minimum Rule which we have written for beginners; and then at length under God's protection you will attain to the loftier heights of doctrine and virtue" (*Rule* 73).

At the Reformation many monasteries were closed or taken over for other purposes, and Benedict's monks were even martyred in those countries where to be a monk was made a capital crime. More of the same occurred with the French Revolution.

But Benedictinism has a habit of reviving. Today about 11,000 men and 22,000 women try to live by the Rule of Benedict in religious communities. Contrary to a popular conception of cloistered Benedictines staying within monastery walls, they have a missionary tradition up to the present time; they are found on every continent. Immediately after the Emancipation Proclamation, Benedictines opened a school for blacks in Savannah, Georgia; for at least a hundred years they have ministered to native Americans in large numbers.

Beginning about a century ago, they were the source of the Liturgical Movement in the Church. Prominent persons beyond the strictly ecclesiastical world have emerged from Benedictine missions and schools: Edward Elgar among musicians and, since World War II, two cabinet ministers in English governments (one Labor, the other Conservative); Senator Eugene McCarthy would certainly affirm that he owes much to his education at Saint John's Abbey, in Collegeville, Minnesota. Outstanding athletes started in their schools: a major league baseball player and a member of England's international rugby team. The best-selling Catholic author in America to date, Thomas Merton, was a monk of Gethsemani Abbey in Kentucky (the Trappists follow a strict interpretation of the Rule of Saint Benedict), diffusing his version of Benedict's vision not just among Roman Catholics. In the 1990's there are four Catholic bishops in the United States who are Benedictine monks; there are two in the United Kingdom, one is the Cardinal Archbishop of Westminster, and both are former abbots of Ampleforth Abbey near York. There are even several communities of Anglican Benedictines. There have been no Benedictine popes in the twentieth century, but there were two in the first half of the nineteenth. Benedict still exerts his influence, even though his sons and daughters are only in a ratio of one to c. 30,000 among the Catholic faithful.

A Note on Inclusive Language

Benedict wrote his rule with his monks in mind. His language usage therefore was not intended to be inclusive. This modern examination of St. Benedict's Rule, while generally opting for inclusive language, respects this historical fact when quoting Benedict.

Julian Stead, O.S.B.

The Life of Saint Benedict

In book 2, chapter 8, of the *Dialogues*, the author indicates his purpose in writing Benedict's life. Saint Gregory's interlocutor, Peter the deacon, interrupts the narrative of Benedict's miracles: "This whole account is really amazing. . . . This man must have been filled with the spirit of all the just" (in particular of Moses, Elisha, Saint Peter, Elijah, and David). Saint Gregory replies, "Actually, Peter, blessed Benedict possessed the Spirit of only one Person, the Savior who fills the hearts of all the faithful by granting them the fruits of his Redemption. For Saint John says of him, 'There is one who enlightens every soul born into the world; he was the true light' (Jn 1:9). And again, 'Of his fullness we have all received' (Jn 1:16)." The purpose of the book therefore is to show how a person filled with the Spirit of Christ does what Christ did (cf. Jn 14:12). *Agere sequitur esse* (actions and deeds are a consequence of what the agent is). The deeds of any true believer in Christ, in whom he dwells, are evidence that Christ himself is omnipotent, omniscient, and ubiquitous.[1]

---

1. All quotations in this chapter are from *Life and Miracles of Saint Benedict* (book 2 of the *Dialogues*) by Gregory the Great, translated by Odo J. Zimmermann, O.S.B. and Benedict R. Avery, O.S.B. (Collegeville: The Liturgical Press, undated). (A small paperback, weighing only 2 oz., which fits easily in a lady's handbag or a gentleman's shirt pocket.)

Some years ago there lived a man who was revered for the holiness of his life. Blessed Benedict was his name, and he was blessed also with God's grace. During his boyhood he showed mature understanding, and a strength of character far beyond his years kept his heart detached from every pleasure. Even while still living in the world, free to enjoy all it had to offer, he saw how empty it was and turned from it without regret.[1]

He was born in Norcia of distinguished parents, who sent him to Rome for a liberal education. When he found many of the students there abandoning themselves to vice, he decided to withdraw from the world he had been preparing to enter; for he was afraid that if he acquired any of its learning he would be drawn down with them to his eternal ruin. In his desire to please God alone, he turned his back on further studies, gave up home and inheritance and resolved to embrace the religious life. He took this step, fully aware of his ignorance; yet he was truly wise, uneducated though he may have been.

(*Life*, Prol.)

Benedict preferred to suffer ill-treatment from the world rather than enjoy its praises. He wanted to spend himself laboring for God, not to be honored by the applause of men. So he stole away . . . and fled to a lonely wilderness about thirty-five miles from Rome, called Subiaco.[2]

At Subiaco, Benedict made his home in a narrow cave and for three years remained concealed there unknown to anyone except the monk Romanus, who lived in a monastery close by. With fatherly concern this monk regularly set aside as much bread as he could from his own portion; then from time to time, unnoticed by his abbot, he left the monastery long enough to take the bread to Benedict.

---

1. Not unlike a modern saint's memories of her childhood: "On the way home I would look up at the stars that shone so quietly, and the sight took me out of myself. . . . I wasn't going to waste any more time looking at an ugly thing like the earth, I would ask Papa to steer me along, and walk with my head well in the air, not looking where I was going. I could gaze forever at that starry vault!" (*Autobiography* of Thérèse of Lisieux, translated by Ronald Knox [New York: P.J. Kenedy and Sons, 1958], p. 67). On pp. 77-78 she describes how she looked on it as a penance when she had to play the games other children played on school holidays. "I was dreadfully bored, especially when I had to spend a whole afternoon dancing quadrilles." Some saints achieve maturity very early.

2. We have told in the Introduction why he stole away and hid from human society.

At length the time came when almighty God wished to reveal Benedict's virtuous life to others, like a shining lamp to give light to everyone in God's house (cf. Mt 5:15). Some shepherds discovered Benedict's hiding place. They recognized in him a servant of God, and many of them gave up their sinful ways for a life of holiness. As a result his name became known to all the people in that locality and great numbers visited his cave, supplying him with the food he needed and receiving from his lips in return spiritual food for their souls.

(Life 1)

One day while the saint was alone, the tempter came in the form of a little blackbird, which began to flutter in front of his face. He made the sign of the cross and the bird flew away. The moment it left, he was seized with an unusually violent temptation. The evil spirit recalled to his mind a woman he had once seen, and before he realized it his emotions were carrying him away. Almost overcome in the struggle, he was on the point of abandoning the lonely wilderness, when suddenly with the help of God's grace he came to himself. He noticed a thick patch of nettles and briers next to him. Throwing his garment aside, he flung himself naked into the sharp thorns and stinging nettles. There he rolled and tossed until his whole body was in pain and covered with blood. Once he had conquered pleasure through suffering, his torn and bleeding skin served to drain off the poison of temptation from his body. Before long the pain that was burning his whole body had put out the fires of evil in his heart. It was by exchanging these two fires that he gained the victory over sin. So complete was his triumph that from then on, as he later told his disciples, he never experienced another temptation of this kind.[1]

Soon after, many forsook the world to place themselves under his guidance, for now that he was free from these temptations he was ready to instruct others in the practice of virtue.

(Life 2)

---

1. A similar tale is told of Francis. Near Assisi there is a garden of roses he rolled in; they bear no thorns and their leaves appear to have blotches of blood on them. Cuttings from these roses grow but with their usual thorns and without the blotches. Francis made a pilgrimage to Subiaco (where the earliest portrait of him is preserved in a mural) and transmitted the same unnatural marks to the bushes in which Benedict took his plunge.

As word spread of his saintly life, the renown of his name increased. One day the entire community of a nearby monastery came to see him. Their abbot had recently died, and they wanted the man of God to be their new superior. For some time he tried to discourage them by refusing, warning them that his way of life would never harmonize with theirs. But they kept insisting until in the end he gave his consent.

He watched carefully over the religious spirit of his monks and would not tolerate any of their previous disobedience. No one was allowed to turn from the straight path of monastic discipline either to the right or to the left. Their waywardness, however, clashed with the standards he upheld, and in their resentment they started to reproach themselves for choosing him as abbot. It only made them the more sullen to find him curbing every fault and evil habit. They could not see why they should have to force their settled minds into new ways of thinking.

At length, proving once again that the very life of the just is a burden to the wicked (cf. Wis 2:12-20), they tried to find a means of doing away with him and decided to poison his wine. A glass pitcher containing this poisoned drink was presented to the man of God during his meal for the customary blessing. As he made the sign of the cross over it with his hand, the pitcher was shattered even though it was well beyond his reach at the time. It broke at his blessing as if he had struck it with a stone.

Then he realized it had contained a deadly drink which could not bear the sign of life. Still calm and undisturbed, he rose at once and after gathering the community together addressed them. "May almighty God have mercy on you," he said. "Why did you conspire to do this? Did I not tell you at the outset that my way of life would never harmonize with yours? Go and find yourselves an abbot to your liking. It is impossible for me to stay here any longer." Then he went back to the wilderness he loved, to live alone with himself in the presence of his heavenly Father.

If he had tried to force them to remain under his rule, he might have forfeited his own fervor and peace of soul and even turned his eyes from the light of contemplation. Their persistent daily faults would have left him almost too weary to correct his own, and he would have been in danger of losing sight of himself without finding them.

Blessed Benedict can be said to have lived *"with himself"* because at all times he kept such close watch over his life and actions. By searching continually into his own soul he always beheld himself in the presence of his

Creator. And this kept his mind from straying. There are two ways we can be carried out of ourselves. Either we fall *below* ourselves through sins of thought, or we are lifted *above* ourselves by the grace of contemplation. The young man who fed the swine sank below himself as a result of his shiftless ways and his unclean life (cf. Lk 15:13-17). The apostle Peter was also out of himself when the angel set him free and raised him to a state of ecstasy, but he was above himself (cf. Acts 12:11). In coming to themselves again, the young man had to break with his sinful past before he could find his true and better self, whereas Saint Peter merely returned from the heights of contemplation to his ordinary state of mind.

Peter asks: Do you think it was right, though, for him to forsake this community, once he had taken it under his care?

Gregory replies: In my opinion, Peter, a superior ought to bear patiently with a community of evil men as long as it has some devout members who can benefit from his presence. When none of the members is devout enough to give any promise of good results, his efforts to help such a community will prove to be a serious mistake, especially if there are opportunities nearby to work more fruitfully for God. Was there anyone the holy man could have hoped to protect by staying where he was, after he saw that they were all united against him? We cannot afford to overlook the attitude of the saints. When they find their work producing no results in one place, they move on to another where it will do some good. This explains the action of the blessed apostle Paul. In order to escape from Damascus, where he was being persecuted, he secured a basket and a rope and had himself secretly lowered over the wall (cf. Acts 9:25). Can we say that Paul feared death, when he expressly declared that he longed to die for the love of Christ? Surely not. But when he saw how little he was accomplishing at Damascus in spite of all his toil, he saved himself for more fruitful labors elsewhere.

As Benedict's influence spread over the surrounding countryside because of his signs and wonders, a great number of men gathered around him to devote themselves to God's service. Christ blessed his work and before long he had established twelve monasteries there, with an abbot and twelve monks in each of them. There were a few other monks whom he kept with him, since he felt that they still needed his personal guidance.

(*Life* 3)

A simple, sincere Goth came to Subiaco to become a monk, and blessed Benedict was very happy to admit him. One day he had him take a brush hook and clear away the briers from a place at the edge of the lake where a garden was to be planted. While the Goth was hard at work cutting down the thick brush, the iron blade slipped off the handle and flew into a very deep part of the lake, where there was no hope of recovering it. At this the poor man ran trembling to Maurus[1] and after describing the accident told him how sorry he was for his carelessness. Maurus in turn informed the servant of God, who went down to the lake, took the handle from the Goth and thrust it in the water. Immediately the iron blade rose from the bottom of the lake and slipped back onto the handle (cf. 4 Kgs 6:4-7). Then he handed the tool back to the Goth and told him, "Continue with your work now. There is no need to be upset."

(Life 6)

The people of that whole region for miles around had grown fervent in their love for Christ, and many of them had forsaken the world in order to bring their hearts under the light yoke of the Savior. In a neighboring church there was a priest named Florentius. Urged on by the bitter enemy of mankind, this priest set out to undermine the saint's work. And, envious as the wicked always are of the holiness in others which they are not striving to acquire themselves, he denounced Benedict's way of life and kept everyone he could from visiting him. The progress of the saint's work, however, could not be stopped. His reputation for holiness kept on growing and with it the number of vocations to a more perfect state of life. This infuriated Florentius all the more. He longed to enjoy the praise the saint was receiving, yet he was unwilling to lead a praiseworthy life himself. At length his soul became so blind with jealousy that he decided to poison a loaf of bread and send it to the servant of God as a sign of Christian fellowship. Though aware at once of the deadly poison it contained, Benedict thanked him for the gift.

At mealtime a raven used to come out of the nearby woods to receive food from the saint's hands. On this occasion he set the poisoned loaf in front of it and said, "In the name of our Lord Jesus Christ, take this bread and carry

---

1. Maurus, son of a pious Roman nobleman, who left him with Benedict to be schooled in the service of God.

it to a place where no one will be able to find it." The raven started to caw and circled around the loaf of bread with open beak and flapping wings as if to indicate that it was willing to obey but found it impossible to do so. Several times the saint repeated the command. "Take the bread," he said, "and do not be afraid! Take it away from here and leave it where no one can find it." The raven finally took the loaf in its beak and flew away. About three hours later, when it had disposed of the bread, it returned and received its usual meal from the hands of the man of God.[1] The saintly abbot now realized how deep his enemy's resentment was and grieved not so much for his own sake as for the priest's. But Florentius, after his failure to do away with the master, determined instead to destroy the souls of the disciples and for this purpose sent seven depraved women into the garden of Benedict's monastery. There they danced together for some time within sight of his followers, in an attempt to lead them into sin. When the saint noticed this from his window, he began to fear that some of his younger monks might go astray. Convinced that the priest's hatred for him was the cause of this attack, he let envy have its way and taking only a few monks with him set out to find a new home. Before he left he reorganized all the monasteries he had founded, adding some new members to the communities.[2]

Hardly had the man of God made his humble escape when almighty God struck the priest down with terrible vengeance. As he was standing on the balcony of his house congratulating himself on Benedict's departure, the structure suddenly collapsed, crushing him to death; yet the rest of the building remained undamaged. This accident occurred before the saint was even ten miles away. His disciple Maurus immediately decided to send a messenger with the news and ask him to return, now that the priest who had caused him so much trouble was dead. Benedict was overcome with sorrow and regret on hearing this, for not only had his enemy been killed but one of his own disciples had rejoiced over his death. And for showing pleasure in sending such a message he gave Maurus a penance to perform.

Although he moved to a different place, his enemy remained the same. The assaults he had to endure after this were all the more violent. . . . The

---

1. Ravens are extremely shy; that Benedict succeeded in taming one is a mark of his being an exceptional person. They still keep a raven or two at Subiaco (in an aviary) to commemorate Benedict's affection for the species.

2. To conclude from this tale that Benedict would not have accepted co-eds in his monastery school would be stretching the point. Fr. Florentius did not send girls as candidates for school but "depraved women."

fortified town of Cassino lies at the foot of a towering mountain. On its summit stood a very old temple, in which the ignorant country people still worshipped Apollo. When the man of God arrived at this spot, he destroyed the idol, overturned the altar and cut down the trees in the sacred groves. Gradually the people of the countryside were won over to the true faith by his zealous preaching. Such losses the ancient enemy could not bear in silence. This time he did not appear to the saint in a dream or under a disguise but face to face. The devil had an utterly revolting appearance. But all these attacks only supplied the saint with further opportunities for victory.

(Life 8)

Meanwhile Benedict began to manifest the spirit of prophecy by foretelling future events and by describing to those who were with him what they had done in his absence.

(Life 11)

It was a custom of the house that monks away on business did not take food or drink outside the monastery.[1] One day a few of them went out on an assignment which kept them occupied till rather late. They stopped for a meal at the house of a devout woman they knew. On their return, when they presented themselves to the abbot for the usual blessing, he asked them where they had taken their meal. "Nowhere," they answered. "Why are you lying to me?" he said. "Did you not enter the house of this particular woman and eat these various foods and have so and so many cups to drink?" On hearing him mention the woman's hospitality and exactly what she had given them to eat and drink, they fell trembling at his feet and confessed their guilt. The man of God did not hesitate to pardon them, confident that they would do no further wrong in his absence, since they now realized he was always present with them in spirit.

(Life 12)

---

1. Cf. *The Rule of Saint Benedict*, 51.

Once while the Goths were still in power Totila their king happened to be marching in the direction of Benedict's monastery. When still some distance away he halted with his troops and sent a messenger ahead to announce his coming, for he had heard that the man of God possessed the gift of prophecy. As soon as he received word that he would be welcome, the crafty king decided to put the saint's prophetic powers to a test. He had Riggo, his sword-bearer, fitted out with royal robes and riding boots and directed him to go in this disguise to the man of God. Three men from his own bodyguard were to march at his side as if he really were the king of the Goths. Totila also provided him with a sword-bearer and other attendants.

As Riggo entered the monastery grounds in his kingly robes and with all his attendants, Benedict caught sight of him and as soon as the company came within hearing called out from where he sat. "Son, lay aside the robes that you are wearing," he said. "They do not belong to you." Aghast at seeing what a great man he had tried to mock, Riggo sank to the ground, and with him all the members of his company. Even after they had risen to their feet they did not dare approach the saint but hurried back in alarm to tell their king how quickly they had been detected.

(Life 14)

King Totila then went to the monastery in person. The moment he noticed the man of God sitting at a distance, he was afraid to come any closer and fell down prostrate where he was. Two or three times Benedict asked him to rise. When Totila still hesitated to do so in his presence, the servant of Christ walked over to him and with his own hands helped him from the ground. Then he rebuked the king for his crimes and briefly foretold everything that was going to happen to him. "You are the cause of many evils," he said. "Put an end now to your wickedness. You will enter Rome and cross the sea. You have nine more years to rule, and in the tenth year you will die." Terrified at these words, the king asked for a blessing and went away. From that time on he was less cruel. Not long after, he went to Rome and then crossed over to Sicily. In the tenth year of his reign he lost his kingdom and his life as almighty God had decreed.

(Life 15)

Under the guidance of Abbot Benedict a nobleman named Theoprobus had embraced monastic life. He was an exemplary religious and had long enjoyed the saint's friendship and confidence. One day on entering Benedict's room he found him weeping bitterly. He asked him what was causing him such sorrow, for he was not weeping as he usually did at prayer but with deep sighs and lamentation. "Almighty God has decreed that this entire monastery and everything I have provided for the community shall fall into the hands of the barbarians," the saint replied. "It was only with the greatest difficulty that I could prevail upon him to spare the lives of its members." This was the prophecy he made to Theoprobus, and we have seen its fulfillment in the recent destruction of his abbey by the Lombards. They came at night while the community was asleep and plundered the entire monastery without capturing a single monk. In this way God fulfilled his promise to Benedict his faithful servant.

(Life 17)

During a time of famine the severe shortage of food was causing a great deal of suffering in Campania. At Benedict's monastery the entire grain supply had been used up and nearly all the bread was gone as well. When mealtime came, only five loaves could be found to set before the community. Noticing how downcast they were, the saint gently reproved them for their lack of trust in God and at the same time tried to raise their dejected spirits with a comforting assurance. "Why are you so depressed at the lack of bread?" he asked. "What if today there is only a little? Tomorrow you will have more than you need." The next day about thirty hundredweights of flour were found in sacks at the gate of the monastery, but no one ever discovered whose services almighty God had employed in bringing them. When they saw what had happened, the monks were filled with gratitude and learned from this miracle that even in their hour of need they must not lose faith in the bountiful goodness of God.

(Life 21)

Some distance from the abbey two women of noble birth were leading the religious life in their own home. A God-fearing layman was kind enough to bring them what they needed from the outside world. Unfortunately, as is sometimes the case, their character stood in sharp contrast to the nobility of their birth, and they were too conscious of their former importance to practice humility toward others. Even under the restraining influence of religious life they still had not learned to control their tongues, and the good layman who served them so faithfully was often provoked at their harsh criticisms. After putting up with their insults for a long time, he went to Benedict and told him how inconsiderate they were. The man of God immediately warned them to curb their sharp tongues and added that he would have to excommunicate them if they did not. This sentence of excommunication was not actually pronounced but only threatened.

A short time afterward the two nuns died without any sign of amendment and were buried in their parish church. Whenever Mass was celebrated, their old nurse, who regularly made an offering for them, noticed that each time the deacon announced, "Everyone who does not receive holy communion must now leave,"[1] these nuns rose from their tombs and went outside. This happened repeatedly until one day she recalled the warning Benedict had given them while they were still alive, when he threatened to deprive them of communion with the Church if they kept on speaking so uncharitably.

The grief-stricken nurse had Abbot Benedict informed of what was happening. He sent her messengers back with an oblation and said, "Have this offered up for their souls during the Holy Sacrifice, and they will be freed from the sentence of excommunication." The offering was made and after that the nuns were not seen leaving the church any more at the deacon's dismissal of the non-communicants. Evidently they had been admitted to communion by our blessed Lord in answer to the prayers of his servant Benedict.

Peter: Is it not extraordinary that souls already judged at God's invisible tribunal could be pardoned by a man who was still living in this mortal flesh, however holy and revered he may have been?

Gregory: What of Peter the apostle? Was he not still living in the flesh when he heard the words, "Whatever thou shalt bind on earth shall be bound in heaven, and whatever thou shalt loose on earth shall be loosed in heaven"

---

1. The deacon's words applied to catechumens and also to the baptized but excommunicated, in the early Church. They are kept today only in the oriental liturgies, before the recitation of the Creed, but their meaning is not always enforced.

(Mt 16:10)? All those who govern the Church in matters of faith and morals exercise the same power of binding and loosing that he received. In fact, the Creator's very purpose in coming down from heaven to earth was to impart to earthly man this heavenly power. It was when God was made flesh for man's sake that flesh received its undeserved prerogative of sitting in judgment even over spirits. What raised our weakness to these heights was the descent of an almighty God to the depths of our own helplessness.

(Life 23)

While Campania was suffering from famine, the holy Abbot distributed food to the needy until there was nothing left in the storeroom but a little oil in a glass vessel. One day when Agapitus, a subdeacon, came to beg for some oil, the man of God ordered the little that remained to be given to him, for he wanted to distribute everything he had to the poor and thus store up riches in heaven (cf. Lk 18:22). The cellarer listened to the abbot's command but did not carry it out. After a while Benedict asked him whether he had given Agapitus the oil. "No," he replied, "I did not. If I had, there would be none left for the community." This angered the man of God, who wanted nothing to remain in the monastery through disobedience, and he told another monk to take the glass with the oil in it and throw it out the window. This time he was obeyed. Even though it struck against the jagged rocks of the cliff below the window, the glass remained intact, and none of the oil had spilled. Abbot Benedict had the glass brought back and given to the subdeacon. Then he sent for the rest of the community and in their presence rebuked the disobedient monk for his pride and lack of faith.

(Life 28)

After that the saint knelt down to pray with his brethren. In the room there happened to be an empty oil-cask. In the course of his prayer the cask gradually filled with oil and the lid started to float on top of it. The next moment the oil was running down the sides of the cask and covering the floor. As soon as he was aware of this, Benedict ended his prayer and the oil stopped flowing. Then turning to the monk who had shown himself disobedient and wanting in confidence, he urged him again to strive to grow in faith and humility.

(Life 29)

One day when he was working in the fields with his monks, a farmer came to the monastery carrying in his arms the lifeless body of his son. Broken-hearted at his loss, he begged to see the saintly abbot and, on learning that he was at work in the fields, left the dead body at the entrance of the monastery and hurried off to find him. By then the abbot was already returning from his work. The moment the farmer caught sight of him he cried out, "Give me back my son! Give me back my son!"

Benedict stopped when he heard this. "But I have not taken your son from you, have I?" he asked. The boy's father only replied, "He is dead. Come! Bring him back to life."

Deeply grieved at his words, the man of God turned to his disciples. "Stand back, brethren!" he said. "Stand back! Such a miracle is beyond our power. The holy apostles are the only ones who can raise the dead (cf. Acts 9:36-41; 20:9-10.) Why are you so eager to accept what is impossible for us?"

But overwhelming sorrow compelled the man to keep on pleading. He even declared with an oath that he would not leave until Benedict restored his son to life. The saint then asked him where the body was. "At the entrance to the monastery," he answered.

When Benedict arrived there with his monks, he knelt down beside the child's body and bent over it. Then rising, he lifted his hands to heaven in prayer. "O Lord," he said, "do not consider my sins but the faith of this man who is asking to see his son alive again, and restore to this body the soul you have taken from it." His prayer was hardly over when the child's whole body began once more to throb with life. No one present there could doubt that this sudden stirring was due to a heavenly intervention. Benedict then took the little boy by the hand and gave him back to his father alive and well.

Obviously, Peter, he did not have the power to work this miracle himself. Otherwise he would not have begged for it prostrate in prayer.

(Life 32)

I must tell you how the saintly Benedict once had a wish he was unable to fulfill. His sister Scholastica, who had been consecrated to God in early childhood, used to visit with him once a year. He would go down to meet her in a house belonging to the monastery a short distance from the entrance.

For this particular visit he joined her there with a few of his disciples and they spent the whole day singing God's praises and conversing about the spiritual life. When darkness was setting in, they took their meal together and continued their conversation until it was quite late. Then the holy nun said to him, "Please do not leave me tonight, brother. Let us keep on talking about the joys of heaven till morning." "What are you saying, sister?" he replied. "You know I cannot stay away from the monastery." The sky was so clear at the time, there was not a cloud in sight. At her brother's refusal Scholastica folded her hands on the table and rested her head upon them in earnest prayer. When she looked up again, there was a sudden burst of lightning and thunder accompanied by such a downpour that Benedict and his companions were unable to set foot outside the door. By shedding a flood of tears while she prayed, this holy nun had darkened the cloudless sky with a heavy rain. The storm began as soon as her prayer was over. In fact, the two coincided so closely that the thunder was already resounding as she raised her head from the table. The very instant she ended her prayer the rain poured down. Realizing that he could not return to the abbey in this terrible storm, Benedict complained bitterly. "God forgive you, sister!" he said. "What have you done?" Scholastica simply answered, "When I appealed to you, you would not listen to me. So I turned to my God and he heard my prayer. Leave now if you can. Leave me here and go back to your monastery." This, of course, he could not do. He had no choice now but to stay. They spent the entire night together and both of them derived great profit from the holy thoughts they exchanged about the interior life.

Here you have my reason for saying that this holy man was once unable to obtain what he desired. If we consider his point of view, we can readily see that he wanted the sky to remain as clear as it was when he came from the monastery. But this wish of his was thwarted by a miracle almighty God performed in answer to a woman's prayer. We need not be surprised that in this instance she proved mightier than her brother; she had been looking forward so long to this visit. Do we not read in Saint John that God is love (1 Jn 4:16)? Surely it is no more than right that her influence was greater than his, since hers was the greater love.

(Life 33)

The next morning Scholastica returned to her convent and Benedict to his monastery. Three days later as he stood in his room looking up toward the sky, he beheld his sister's soul leaving her body and entering the heavenly court in the form of a dove. Overjoyed at her eternal glory, he gave thanks to God in hymns of praise. Then, after informing his brethren of her death, he sent some of them to bring her body to the abbey and bury it in the tomb he had prepared for himself. The bodies of these two were now to share a common resting place, just as in life their souls had always been one in God.

(*Life* 34)

At another time the deacon Servandus came to see the servant of God on one of his regular visits. He was abbot of a monastery in Campania and always welcomed an opportunity to discuss with Benedict the truths of eternity, for he, too, was a man of deep spiritual understanding. In speaking of their hopes and longings they were able to taste in advance the heavenly food that was not yet fully theirs to enjoy. When it was time to retire for the night, Benedict went to his room on the second floor of the tower, leaving Servandus in the one below, which was connected with his own by a stairway.

Long before the Night Office began, the man of God was standing at his window, where he watched and prayed while the rest were still asleep. In the dead of night he suddenly beheld a flood of light shining down from above more brilliant than the sun, and with it every trace of darkness cleared away. Another remarkable sight followed. According to his own description, the whole world was gathered up before his eyes in what appeared to be a single ray of light. He called out for Servandus; Servandus rushed to the upper room and was just in time to catch a final glimpse of the miraculous light.

Keep this well in mind, Peter. All creation is bound to appear small to a soul that sees the Creator. Once it beholds a little of his light, it finds all creatures small indeed. The light of holy contemplation enlarges and expands the mind in God until it stands above the world. In fact, the soul that sees him rises even above itself, and as it is drawn upward in his light all its inner powers unfold.

In saying that the world was gathered up before his eyes, I do not mean that heaven and earth grew small but that his spirit was enlarged. Absorbed as he was in God, it was now easy for him to see all that lay beneath God. In the light outside that was shining before his eyes, there was a brightness which reached into his mind and lifted his spirit heavenward, showing him the insignificance of all that lies below.

(*Life* 35)

Six days before he died he gave orders for his tomb to be opened. Almost immediately he was seized with a violent fever that rapidly wasted his remaining energy. Each day his condition grew worse until finally on the sixth day he had his disciples carry him into the chapel, where he received the body and blood of our Lord to gain strength for his approaching end. Then, supporting his weakened body on the arms of his brethren, he stood with his hands raised to heaven and as he prayed breathed his last. That day two monks, one of them at the monastery, the other some distance away, received the very same revelation. They both saw a magnificent road covered with rich carpeting and glittering with thousands of lights. From his monastery it stretched eastward in a straight line until it reached up into heaven. And there in the brightness stood a man of majestic appearance, who asked them, "Do you know who passed this way?" "No," they replied. "This," he told them, "is the road taken by blessed Benedict, the Lord's beloved, when he went to heaven."

His body was laid to rest in the chapel of Saint John the Baptist, which he had built to replace the altar of Apollo.

(*Life* 37)

Even in the cave at Subiaco, where he had lived before, this holy man still works numerous miracles for people who turn to him with faith and confidence. The incident I am going to relate happened only recently. A woman who had completely lost her mind was roaming day and night over hills and valleys, through forests and fields, resting only when she was utterly exhausted. One day in the course of her aimless wanderings she strayed into the saint's cave and rested there without the least idea of where she was. The next morning she woke up entirely cured and left the cave without even a trace of her former affliction. After that she remained free from it for the rest of her life.

(*Life* 38)

With all the renown he gained by his numerous miracles, the holy man was no less outstanding for the wisdom of his teaching. He wrote a Rule for Monks that is remarkable for its discretion and its clarity of language. Anyone who wishes to know more about his life and character can discover in his Rule exactly what he was like as an abbot, for his life could not have differed from his teaching.

(*Life* 36)

* * *

In the rest of this book we will consider excerpts from Benedict's Rule. We shall begin with his instructions to the abbot, because they represent the kind of man he tried to be. He did not write a portrait of the ideal monk, perhaps because individuals are so different that it would be impossible to devise a pattern suitable for all. He seems to have thought that the success of a monastery would depend greatly on what kind of man the abbot is. If he corresponds to the model, he may be able to get the best out of each of his monks and keep them together. If he does not, there will be trouble.

Benedict's guidelines for an abbot are of value to Christians in a position of leadership: to an officer in the military, for instance, or to a school principal, the director of a company, and not least to the mother or father of a family.

The Abbot

An abbot who is worthy to be over a monastery must always remember what his title signifies and act as a superior should. For he is believed to hold the place of Christ in the monastery, being called by a title of his, taken from the words of the apostle: "You have received a Spirit of adoption of sons, through which we cry, 'Abba'— (that is, 'Father'!)" (Rom 8:15). Therefore the abbot ought not to teach or ordain or command anything which is against the Lord's precepts; on the contrary, his commands and his teaching should be a leaven of divine justice kneaded into the minds of his disciples. (*Rule* 2)[1]

Christ is the only teacher (cf. Mt 23:8). A Christian in a position of leadership will bear in mind that he must be as Christ to his subordinates: a representative of God's fatherhood, a strict but fair judge, a healer, a teacher, a good shepherd. Admittedly, this is an impossible ideal to achieve, humanly speaking. It is also humbling to have a divine model to try to live up to; one has to trust in Christ's willingness to fill up by grace what is lacking to human wisdom and power, that the Spirit of Christ will make up for the limits to one's own talents. To think that they could be sufficient of themselves would be presumptuous. But the principle is only an application to a leader's responsibilities of 1 John 2:1-6, which tells us to live as Christ lived (plus John 15:5, "I am the vine, you are the branches"). Leaders have to be themselves and yet empty themselves to make room for Christ. A leader therefore will guard himself against "ordaining or commanding anything contrary to the Lord's precepts," in cases where there is no explicit directive from the words of the Lord.

---

1. Our quotations from the Rule are mostly taken from *St. Benedict's Rule for Monasteries* (abbreviated *Rule*), translated from the Latin by Leonard J. Doyle (Collegeville: The Liturgical Press, 1948). This is a handy little paperback, like the *Life and Miracles of Saint Benedict*, and it is a good translation. A more modern translation, by a group of scholars, from the same publisher, is *RB 1980: The Rule of Saint Benedict,* obtainable either in a small paperback with no commentary, or a hardback edition, which includes the Latin original and excellent commentaries along with the addresses of the fifty-odd monasteries in North America which belong to the Benedictine Confederation.

Let the abbot always bear in mind that at the dread Judgment of God there will be an examination of these two matters: his teaching and the obedience of his disciples. And let the abbot be sure that any lack of profit the master of the house may find in the sheep will be laid to the blame of the shepherd. On the other hand, if the shepherd has bestowed all his pastoral diligence on a restless, unruly flock and tried every remedy for their unhealthy behavior, then he will be acquitted at the Lord's Judgment and may say to the Lord with the prophet: "I have not concealed your justice within my heart; your truth and your salvation I have declared. But they have despised and rejected me." And then finally let death itself swallow up the sheep who were disobedient to his care. (*Rule* 2)

Today we hear a lot about "the judgment of history"—really the judgment of historians, feared despite their limitations, prejudices, and fallibility. That is not the judgment which Benedict would have us "always bear in mind," whether or not we are comforted at the thought that Christ's judgment will be more fair. The fear of divine judgment permeates the Rule, calling to mind one of those great mosaics dominating the whole interior of ancient churches or basilicas from the apse, depicting *Christ Pantocrator* (All-Sovereign). The reader may have difficulty with this; it may seem to clash with Benedict's equal insistence on mutual love between the soul and God, initiated by the merciful Lord himself. It would be consistent with scripture (particularly the Song of Songs) to make the following comparison: in this life we are not yet permanently united with God. Our relationship with him is not so similar to the indissoluble bond of marriage as to that of an engaged couple, committed but not irrevocably. If there was true love between a woman and her fiance, she would fear to commit any infidelity which might cause a breach between them.

An awesome sense of Jesus as both judge and lover is expressed in the hymns of the Benedictine liturgy for the Feast of the Lord's Ascension: "What clemency overcame you, to make you undertake to bear the burden of our sins and suffer a cruel death in order to rescue us from death! . . . Death is dissolved in the triumph of grace, as you climb to the tribunal (or judgment seat) at the right hand of the Father."[1]

---

1. Quae te vicit clementia, Ut ferres nostra crimina,
   Crudelem mortem patiens, Ut nos a morte tolleres!
   . . . Quo mors soluta deperit, Datur triumphus gratiae:
   Scandens tribunal dexterae Patris.

There is not lacking a sense of Christ as also our advocate, expressed in these words of the Letter to the Hebrews: "Surely he did not come to help angels but rather the children of Abraham; therefore he had to become like his brothers in every way, that he might be a merciful and faithful high priest before God on their behalf, to expiate the sins of the people. Since he was himself tested through what he suffered, he is able to help those who are tempted" (Heb 2:16-18).

Benedict compared the souls entrusted to his care to sheep which their owner, who had bred them, entrusted to him as their shepherd. He must profit them, benefit them; and since he must see to their growth and their health, he is also like a physician in their regard.

One needs to be wary of reading into ancient texts the concepts of later cultures, for instance those of postfreudian psychology. But a certain fore-shadowing or anticipation of those concepts is discernible in Benedict's model abbot, a person similar to a professional therapist in our world, that is, willing to listen to the confidences of others about their wounded or negative feelings, with a view to healing them. The abbot is expected to have experienced monks on his staff, who can assist in this important function; psychotherapy presupposes a particular kind of ability in the therapist, akin to what theology calls "the discernment of spirits." The abbot is certainly not required to be an accredited psychiatrist. No; Benedict did not expect his monastery to be, in effect, a mental hospital. But he expected his monastery to accept into its brotherhood any man who showed the seriousness of his desire by his persistence in seeking entry:

> When anyone is newly come for the reformation of his life, let him not be granted an easy entrance; but, as the apostle says, "Test the spirits to see whether they are from God." If the newcomer, therefore, perseveres in his knocking on the door, and if it is seen after four or five days that he bears patiently the . . . difficulty of admission, and that he persists in his petition, then let entrance be granted him, and let him stay in the guest house for a few days. After that let him be in the quarters for the novices, where they study, eat and sleep. A senior shall be assigned to them who is skilled in winning souls, to watch over them with the utmost care. Let him examine whether the novice is truly seeking God, and whether he is zealous for the Work of God [prayer], for obedience and for humiliations. Let the novice be told all the hard and rugged ways

by which the journey to God is made. . . . At the end of two months let this Rule be read through to him, and let him be addressed thus: "Here is the law under which you wish to fight. If you can observe it, enter; if you cannot, you are free to depart." If he still stands firm, let him be taken to the above-mentioned novitiate and again tested in all patience. (*Rule* 58)

After the lapse of another six months, and again after four months more, the Rule is again read to him,

> that he may know on what he is entering. Then, having deliberated within himself, if he promises to keep it in its entirety and to observe everything that is commanded him, let him be received into the community. (*Rule* 58)

Common sense, as well as belief in original sin, tells us that a fair number will bring with them an inherited burden from past sins and past negative experiences, resulting in character defects and emotional weaknesses. These need to be healed, and the chief healer should be the abbot himself. During the year in the novitiate, it is presumed that some will find their weaknesses are such that they could not endure the yoke of the monastic Rule the rest of their lives. They are free to depart.

Reading between the lines of the Rule, one discerns that Benedict met a good deal of suffering in his monastery, and not just from physical hardships. An historical novel could be written on the basis of the vices and emotional temperaments he seems to have had to deal with. He saw it as every abbot's principal duty to use all the means at his disposal to help the sufferers and/or sinners to enter eternal life with the saints, "now cleansed from vice and sin" (*Rule* 7).

> Let the abbot be most solicitous in his concern for delinquent brethren, for "it is not the healthy but the sick who need a physi- cian." And therefore he ought to use every means that a wise physician would use. Let him send "senpectae," that is, brethren of mature years and wisdom, who may as it were secretly console the wavering brother and induce him to make humble satisfaction; comforting him that he may not be "overcome by excessive grief" (2 Cor 2:7), but that, as the apostle says, charity may be strengthened in him. And let everyone pray for him. (*Rule* 27)

Vatican II's decree on the renewal of religious life, which henceforth we will quote under its Latin title *Perfectae Caritatis*, reflects Benedict's mind: "Let each superior, as one who will render an account of the souls entrusted to him, use his authority in a spirit of service for the brethren and manifest thereby the charity with which God loves them" (#14).

> For the abbot must have the utmost solicitude and exercise all prudence and diligence lest he lose any of the sheep entrusted to him. Let him know that what he has undertaken is the care of weak souls and not a tyranny over strong ones; and let him fear the prophet's warning through which God says, "What you saw to be fat you took to yourselves, and what was feeble you cast away." Let him rather imitate the loving example of the Good Shepherd who left the ninety-nine sheep in the mountains and went to look for the one sheep that had gone astray, on whose weakness he had such compassion that he deigned to place it on his own sacred shoulders and thus carry it back to the flock. (*Rule* 27)

The Abbot As Teacher

Some children are endowed from birth with such intelligence that they have no great need for a good school or teachers; given a good library and, for a scientist, good laboratory facilities, once they have learned the rudiments they can largely educate themselves. It is the more limited minds that need a good school, with teachers who can understand and help them overcome their difficulties and give them encouragement. This is true in the spiritual order as well, in learning to acquire moral strength; it is the weak that Benedict wants to help; he wishes the abbot to be a role model for them; they can be inspired better by example than by words; they can follow the example they see, better than rules which may only discourage them. When they see a living example, they may say, "If you can do it, so can I."

Like an ideal father, the abbot must love his wayward children, tempering discipline with mercy, sobriety, and understanding.

> Therefore, when anyone receives the name of abbot, he ought to govern his disciples with a twofold teaching. That is to say, he should show them all that is good and holy by his deeds even more than by his words, expounding the Lord's commandments in words

to the intelligent among his disciples, but demonstrating the divine precepts by his actions for those of harder hearts and ruder minds. And whatever he has taught his disciples to be contrary to God's law, let him indicate by his example that it is not to be done, lest, while preaching to others, he himself be found reprobate, and lest God one day say to him in his sin, "Why do you declare my statutes and profess my covenant with your lips, whereas you hate discipline and have cast my words behind you?" And again, "You were looking at the speck in your brother's eye and did not see the beam in your own." (*Rule* 2)

Toward the end of his Rule, in the chapter "On Constituting an Abbot," Benedict enlarges on this concept of the abbot as a teacher:

Merit of life and wisdom of doctrine should determine the choice of the one to be constituted, even if he be the last in the order of the community. . . . Let them set a worthy steward over the house of God. Once he has been constituted, let the abbot always bear in mind what a burden he has undertaken and to whom he will have to give an account of his stewardship, and let him know that his duty is rather to profit his brethren than to preside over them. He must therefore be learned in the divine law, that he may have a treasure of knowledge from which to bring forth new things and old. He must be chaste, sober and merciful. Let him exalt mercy above judgment, that he himself may obtain mercy. He should hate vices; he should love the brethren.

In administering correction he should act prudently and not go to excess, lest in seeking too eagerly to scrape off the rust he break the vessel. Let him keep his own frailty ever before his eyes and remember that the bruised reed must not be broken. By this we do not mean that he should allow vices to grow; on the contrary, as we have already said, he should eradicate them prudently and with charity, in the way which may seem best in each case. Let him study rather to be loved than to be feared.

Let him not be excitable and worried, nor exacting and headstrong, nor jealous and over-suspicious; for then he is never at rest.

In his commands let him be prudent and considerate; and whether the work which he enjoins concerns God or the world, let him be discreet and moderate, bearing in mind the discretion of holy Jacob, who said, "If I cause my flocks to be overdriven, they will all die in one day." Taking this, then, and other examples of discretion, the mother of virtues, let him so temper all things that the strong may have something to strive after, and the weak may not fall back in dismay. (*Rule* 64)

Back to chapter 2:

Let him make no distinction of persons in the monastery. Let him not love one more than another, unless it be one whom he finds better in good works or in obedience. Let him not advance one of noble birth ahead of one who was formerly a slave, unless there be some other reasonable ground for it. But if the abbot for just reason thinks fit to do so, let him advance one of any rank whatever. Otherwise let them keep their due places; because, whether slaves or freemen, we are all one in Christ and bear an equal burden of service in the army of the same Lord. For with God there is no respect of persons. Only for one reason are we preferred in his sight: if we be found better than others in good works and humility. Therefore let the abbot show equal love to all and impose the same discipline on all according to their deserts. (*Rule* 2)

Nothing can make an abbot lose his brothers' respect like favoritism. He has to be very careful not to let his heart rule his head, especially when it comes to choosing advisers and conferring honors and responsibilities. Parents of a large family must also try to love each one equally; it hurts a child to feel he or she is unwanted, or less appreciated than others.

Benedict is impressed by nothing but Christ-like behavior, whether in the simple monk or in the abbot himself: "We are all one in Christ and bear an equal burden of service in the army of the same Lord." The task of an army is a matter of life and death, and so is a monastery's: the life and death of souls. When it comes to actual battle, what counts then is how well the individual carries out orders or handles his weapon. Chapter 4, on "The Instruments of Good Works," lists the monk's armory.

As a practical example of the point, the abbot may have a monk to whom he is not personally attracted; he is a bore in conversation, and his fortune is certainly not his face or his physique. But the abbot has learned from experience that this monk will do anything he is asked and is reliably present at his duties. If asked to teach third year French (present day monasteries often run schools or colleges), he will do it, keeping a page or two ahead of the class, even though he and the abbot know he has no college or even high school credits in French. But he picked up some French once somehow—not enough to really teach it well, and he is well aware that others could do it better. But a monk like that can be depended on, like a box of spare parts, to fill arising needs satisfactorily. In fact he will do several jobs at once like that. Benedict will allow the abbot to love such a man more than others, "because he is better in good works and obedience/humility." Another monk may be more admirable for his advanced education, but the abbot knows he cannot rely on him to do what he is not interested in for the moment.

Another may be more entertaining but again not reliable when it comes to thankless or unrewarding jobs. It is prayer and hard work, rather than keeping the abbot and community amused, that the house of God must depend upon, if it is to thrive.

Another may be "of noble birth." But it is what *he* is, not what his ancestors were, that should earn the abbot's respect. It is scandalous if a monk who was a "slave" (we would say today "of a poor family") is taken advantage of and overburdened, while various privileges are given another because he is from a distinguished or wealthy family—which might reward the abbey materially for special honor shown to its son.

And as for good looks, Benedict is aware that they are fleeting and superficial; being a realist, he warns the abbot not to be too impressed or attracted to anything in a monk but "good works and obedience/humility." He might have had Luke 1:48 in the back of his mind: it seems to have been for her *humility* that God preferred Mary above all other women, so that "all ages to come" would "call her blessed."

In his teaching the abbot should always follow the apostle's formula: "Reprove, entreat, rebuke"; he must adapt himself to circumstances, now using severity and now persuasion, showing now the stern countenance of a master, now the loving affection of a father. That is to say, it is the undisciplined and restless whom he must reprove rather sharply; it is the obedient, meek and patient whom he must entreat to advance in virtue; while as for the negligent and disdainful, these we charge him to rebuke and correct.

And let him not shut his eyes to the faults of offenders; but, since he has the authority, let him cut out those faults by the roots as soon as they begin to appear, remembering the fate of Eli, the priest of Shiloh [cf. 1 Sam 2-4]. The well-disposed and those of good understanding let him correct with verbal admonition the first and second time. But bold, hard, proud and disobedient characters he should curb at the very beginning of their ill-doing by stripes and other bodily punishments, knowing that it is written, "The fool is not corrected with words," and again, "Beat your son with the rod and you will deliver his soul from death." (*Rule* 2)

Benedict values stability (the ability to be faithful to commitments) and order; their opposites are restlessness, chaos, negligence—marks of an unhealthy society or individual. The spirit of obedience (we might call that "cooperation" today), evangelical meekness and patience are the virtues needed to preserve stability and order.

The abbot cannot always be "Mr. Nice Guy," though he "study rather to be loved than to be feared." Sometimes it is better for his subordinates that he make himself feared, though disliked; it is *their* good that he must put first, and *Christ's* judgment upon him that he must fear, not theirs.

The abbot should always remember what he is and what he is called, and should know that to whom more is committed, from him more is required. Let him understand also what a difficult and arduous task he has undertaken: ruling souls and adapting himself to a variety of characters. One he must coax, another scold, another persuade, according to each one's character and understanding. Thus he must adjust and adapt himself to all in such a way that he may not only suffer no loss in the flock committed to his care but may even rejoice in the increase of a good flock. (*Rule* 2)

Even for Benedict, it was an uphill road. As Paul and Barnabas told the faithful in Antioch, shortly after Paul had been stoned and left for dead in Iconium, "We must undergo many trials if we are to enter into the reign of God" (Acts 14:22).

Above all let him not neglect or undervalue the welfare of the souls committed to him, in a greater concern for fleeting, earthly, perishable things; but let him always bear in mind that he has undertaken the government of souls and that he will have to give an account of them. And if he be tempted to allege a lack of earthly means, let him remember what is written: "First seek the kingdom of God and his justice, and all these things shall be given you besides." And again: "Nothing is wanting to those who fear him."

Let him know, then, that he who has undertaken the government of souls must prepare himself to render an account of them. Whatever number of brethren he knows he has under his care, he may be sure beyond doubt that on Judgment Day he will have to give the Lord an account of all these souls, as well as of his own soul. Thus the constant apprehension about his coming examination as shepherd concerning the sheep entrusted to him, and his anxiety over the account that must be given for others, make him careful of his own record. And while by his admonitions he is helping others to amend, he himself is cleansed of his faults. (*Rule* 2)

The pages devoted to the abbot portray what kind of man Benedict found he needed to be (his ideal for himself), and we have tried to indicate how valuable his principles remain for us, if we are in an analogous position. More will appear, regarding how the abbot should be seen in the eyes of his subjects, in the next chapter (on the Prologue to the Rule), in the chapters on Humility, and the chapter on Community.

The Prologue to the Rule

Following the chapter on the master, it is fitting to present excerpts from the initial address to the disciple:

> Listen, my son, to your master's precepts, and incline the ear of your heart. Receive willingly and carry out effectively your loving father's advice, that by the labor of obedience you may return to him from whom you had departed by the sloth of disobedience. (*Rule*, Prol.)

The English word "obedience" implies something slavish. It has not that connotation in the Latin language, much less in Benedict's spirituality. It is derived from the word meaning "to hear, to listen to (and heed) someone's voice." *Perfectae Caritatis* expresses the ideal of religious obedience as a way people choose "to follow Christ *more freely*, dedicated to God, and to devote themselves in a special way to the Lord" (#1).

"The master" and "loving father" whom Benedict bids his son to heed, has several layers of meaning. First, of course, it means the author and text of the Rule; but also God, speaking through Benedict and through one's abbot (cf. the previous chapter). As it refers to God, it means both Christ, the incarnate Word of God, who speaks to us through holy scripture (the word of God in book form), and the Spirit of Christ, whom we do not need to invite into our hearts, because he is already there. We are urged to tune into him.

"The labor of obedience" is seen as the opposite of the disobedience of our first parents and the way to retrace our steps out of the mess into which they unfortunately plunged their progeny. Be obedient, rather than stray farther from God by choosing to imitate their mistake.

These concepts permeate the whole Rule and are singularly apposite for this decade of "the new evangelization": Benedict is inviting us to "evangelize" ourselves, "inclining the ear of one's heart" constantly to the word of God, expressed in the gospel of Jesus Christ, in all the scriptures, even in the laws of all legitimate authority, and last but not least in the depths of one's own soul.

To you, therefore, my words are now addressed, whoever you may be, who are renouncing your own will to do battle under the Lord Christ, the true King, and are taking up the strong, bright weapons of obedience.

In a good many places (cf. *Rule* 1, 58, 61) Benedict uses military language, as does the New Testament (cf. 2 Cor 10:3; Ja 4:1; 1 Pt 2:11; Rv 2:16; 12:7; 17:14; 19:11). We do not wish to deny the good motives of those who thought up the ideal of "the Christian knight," but it was not Benedict's, nor what he meant by "doing battle under the Lord Christ"; nothing was farther from his peaceful mind. However noble that ideal may have been originally, it has led to violence, millions of deaths, even between Christians who wished to defend or impose on others their differing interpretations of the gospel: and we are still suffering the consequences, wars and terrorism stemming from ethnic hatred and fears that originated in religious wars. They cannot be laid at Benedict's door.

It is by "renouncing our own will" that we make the transition from a spoiled child to maturity. For this purpose discipline, military discipline for instance, is recognized by many as beneficial to the young.

To love God in the depths of our hearts, choosing his will as our first, and in a sense our *only* good, is after all the first of the Ten Commandments transmitted by Moses. While being reminded of that, let us not forget either that it includes a radical love of our neighbor as its expression (cf. *Rule* 71, 72). All that Benedict teaches about obedience has as its goal the facilitating of the love of God.

God's will is as mysterious as God himself, as beautiful as his face, identical with his love. Therefore it is not something to which we just resign ourselves. The Blessed Virgin, in one of her few recorded statements, expressed the proper attitude to it: "Be it done unto me according to your word." By her humble assent to God's will, from one moment to another, she carried out God's plan for her. If—like her—we will have done God's will, we will discover some day what place God reserved for us in history, and we will occupy the place he prepared in heaven for us alone. This is not something we should *resign* ourselves to; it is what we should joyfully *seek*. It is the most intelligent thing for us to do.

It would not be inappropriate to interrupt the Prologue here with more of Benedict's teaching on obedience:

The first degree of humility is obedience without delay. This is the virtue of those who hold nothing dearer to them than Christ; who, because of the holy service they have professed, and the fear of hell, and the glory of life everlasting, as soon as anything has been ordered by the superior, receive it as a divine command and cannot suffer any delay in executing it. Of these the Lord says, "As soon as he heard, he obeyed me." (*Rule* 5)

In its own words, *Perfectae Caritatis* says the same: "Under the influence of the Holy Spirit, religious submit themselves to their superiors, whom faith presents as God's representatives, and through whom they are guided into the service of all their brothers in Christ" (#14).

Such as these, therefore, immediately leaving their own affairs and forsaking their own will, dropping the work they were engaged in and leaving it unfinished, with the ready step of obedience follow up with their deeds the voice of him who commands. . . . The disciple's work is completed in the swiftness of the fear of God by those who are moved with the desire of attaining life everlasting. That desire is their motive for choosing the narrow way, of which the Lord says, "Narrow is the way that leads to life," so that, not living according to their own choice nor obeying their own desires and pleasures but walking by another's judgment and command, they dwell in monasteries and desire to have an abbot over them. Assuredly such as these are living up to that maxim of the Lord in which he says, "I have come not to do my own will but the will of him who sent me." (*Rule* 5)

Of religious, *Perfectae Caritatis* says: "The more ardently they unite themselves to Christ through a self-surrender involving their entire lives, the more vigorous becomes the life of the Church and the more abundantly her apostolate bears fruit" (#1).

But this very obedience will be acceptable to God and pleasing to men only if what is commanded is done without hesitation, delay, lukewarmness, grumbling, or objection. For the obedience given to superiors is given to God, since he himself has said, "He who hears you, hears me." And the disciples should offer their obedience with a good will, for "God loves a cheerful giver." If the disciple obeys with an ill-will and murmurs, not necessarily with his lips but simply in his heart, then even though he fulfil the command, yet his work will not be acceptable to God, who sees that his heart is murmuring. And far from gaining a reward for such work as this, he will incur the punishment due to murmurers, unless he amend and make satisfaction. (*Rule 5*)

Chapter 5, just quoted, is a condensation of a much longer chapter in the Rule of the Master (cf. Introduction) and contains elements of earlier monastic tradition, for example, the monks of Egypt quoted by John Cassian. Original and therefore especially characteristic of Benedict, is chapter 71, "That the Brethren Be Obedient to One Another," showing the supreme importance he attached to mutual charity and unity among brothers:

Not only is the boon of obedience to be shown by all to the abbot, but the brethren are also to obey one another, knowing that by this road of obedience they are going to God. Giving priority, therefore, to the commands of the abbot and of the superiors appointed by him (to which we allow no private orders to be preferred), for the rest let all the juniors obey their seniors with all charity and solicitude. But if anyone is found contentious, let him be corrected. (*Rule 71*)

Orderliness, as in the pecking order of authority, is typical of Benedict; it is one way of safeguarding peace in a community.

And if any brother, for however small a cause, is corrected in any way by the abbot or by any of his superiors, or if he faintly perceives that the mind of any superior is angered or moved against him, however little, let him at once, without delay, prostrate himself on the ground at his feet and lie there making satisfaction until that emotion is quieted with a blessing. But if anyone should disdain to do this, let him undergo corporal punishment or, if he is stubborn, let him be expelled from the monastery. (*Rule 71*)

The almost acrobatic way of restoring good will belongs to another time and culture than ours, as does corporal punishment; we may find those details repugnant, but the penalty of expulsion, no matter how long the proud brother may have been in the community or how valuable his work may be, reflects an uncompromising insistence on peace and unity in a Christian community, and on humility and universal good will in its individual members. To continue with the Prologue:

> We must always so serve him with the good things he has given us, that he will never as an angry Father disinherit his children . . . who would not follow him to glory. Let us arise, then, at last, for the scripture stirs us up, saying, "Now is the hour for us to rise from sleep." Let us open our eyes to the deifying light, let us hear with attentive ears the warning which the divine voice cries daily to us, "Today if you hear his voice, harden not your hearts." And again, "He who has ears to hear, let him hear what the Spirit says to the churches: 'Come, my children, listen to me; I will teach you the fear of the Lord. Run while you have the light of life, lest the darkness of death overtake you.' "

Benedict sounds almost like an athletic coach in his insistence on living in the present moment with the utmost energy; this, and also the importance of listening to the inner voice of the Spirit, is a classic principle of the spiritual life. *Perfectae Caritatis* echoes Benedict's metaphor of monastic life as a response to the divine voice: "Members of each community should recall above everything else that by their profession of the evangelical counsels [poverty, chastity, and obedience; cf. Mt 19:10-12, 21] they have given answer to a divine call to live for God alone" (#1).

> God says to you, "If you will have true and everlasting life, keep your tongue from evil and your lips that they speak no guile. Turn away from evil and do good; seek after peace and pursue it. And when you have done these things, my eyes shall be upon you and my ears open to your prayers; and before you call upon me, I will say to you, 'Behold, here I am.' " What can be sweeter to us, dear brethren, than this voice of the Lord inviting us? Behold, in his loving kindness the Lord shows us the way of life. (*Rule,* Prol.)

"Keep your tongue from evil": Benedict is very strong on holding one's tongue. The Trappist reform of the Cistercian Order went so far as to allow monks only sign language, except for communicating with their superior or confessor. It has been said that silence is not a Christian virtue, Jesus having told his disciples to preach to all humankind. However, experience has shown that speech is not the only way to preach; many well-meaning Christians attempt it without really having the charism or education necessary. They cause more annoyance than edification, having nothing appropriate or significant to say. There are people who talk for the sake of talking, compulsively; it can be very annoying, especially when one is trying to maintain a spirit of prayer and listen to the voice of God. The following true story exemplifies this: A client came to a lawyer, saying he wanted a divorce. The lawyer asked him, "Why?" "My wife talks too much." "What does she talk about?" "That's just it—she don't say!"

This can be a form of noise pollution: an object sometimes of fanatical opposition. There was a confessor to a religious community who gave all the nuns the same advice: "Do it *quietly*, mother." Not bad advice for keeping order in a classroom, working with others in an office, even for life at home. There is another case of a certain monk who returned to his monastery after going astray. He had planned to marry a widow, but he could not stand all the noise made by her teenage children. They helped him tremendously to appreciate the relative value of the quiet he had left. (Benedict says a monk who leaves should be received back, up to three times.)

Shakespeare too was sympathetic to the ideal of quiet and silence: "Where words are scarce they are seldom spent in vain," says a wise man in Richard II; and Polonius in Hamlet advises his son, "Give every man thine ear but few thy voice." One way to love others is to let them have the first word; it is a way to show them honor, to "obey" (=listen to them). A humble person approaches others empty of self, putting himself or herself at their disposal, enabling them to express themselves, as they find him or her receptive. A humble person will take a real interest in what *others* have to say. This is the attitude Benedict wants in a monk; it can be extended to others, for the sake of their neighbor. By allowing him or her to speak freely and openly, revealing their inner self, one may be able to respond with more appropriate truths, perhaps of the gospel, which may enlighten them. This is a good way to approach others affected by materialism, practical atheism, and religious indifference, if we wish to make a contribution toward the world's re-evangelization.

Here are Benedict's words on "The Spirit of Silence":

Let us do what the prophet [David, the author of the psalms] says:
"I said, 'I will guard my ways, that I may not sin with my tongue.

I have set a guard to my mouth.' I was mute and was humbled, and
kept silence even from good things. " Here the prophet shows that
if the spirit of silence ought to lead us at times to refrain even from
good speech, so much the more ought the punishment for sin make
us avoid evil words.

Therefore, since the spirit of silence is so important, permission
to speak should rarely be granted even to perfect disciples, even
though it be for good, holy, edifying conversation; for it is written,
"In much speaking you will not escape sin," and in another place,
"Death and life are in the power of the tongue." For speaking and
teaching belong to the master; the disciple's part is to be silent and
to listen.

And for that reason if anything has to be asked of the superior, it
should be asked with all the humility and submission inspired by
reverence.

But as for coarse jests and idle words or words that move to
laughter, these we condemn everywhere with a perpetual ban, and
for such conversation we do not permit a disciple to open his mouth.
(*Rule* 6)

Benedict's views on humor are in tune with other Church Fathers; see, for
example, the Patriarch Photios' advice to Boris Michael, the first Christian
ruler of Bulgaria: "Ribaldry has hurt many persons; for, even if born in jest,
it becomes a mortal blow to those ridiculed; it may bring fleeting pleasure to
those involved, but it produces many enmities among the serious-minded.
Every man, but especially the ruler, should stand on his guard against it,
because it is vulgar and is judged contemptible rather than witty."[1]

Some people can use humor for a serious purpose; perhaps Benedict
would have been more lenient in their case. But he does not seem to consider
humor generally compatible with reverence for the presence of God, as
Photios considered it incompatible with charity.

Two other points remain to be made, from the last text quoted from the
Prologue: first, "Keep . . . your lips that they speak no guile." We will have
more to say about this, when we comment on "The Instruments of Good

---

1. Despina Stratoudaki White and Joseph R. Berrigan, Jr., *The Patriarch and the
   Prince, The Letter of Patriarch Photios of Constantinople to Khan Boris of
   Bulgaria* (Brookline: The Holy Cross Orthodox Press, 1982), p. 75, #101.

Works" (*Rule* 4). The other point is belief in the presence of God. There will be more to say about that too, both when we examine more particulars in his teaching on humility, and relative to Christ's promise to be present "wherever two or three come together in my name" (Mt 18:20), a presence of which Benedict taught we must be especially aware at the place and time of liturgical prayer. Without this awareness, monastic life could be unbearably lonely, and there would be little sense in living in a community rather than on one's own. Without this awareness, community life might not lead to Christian perfection but to a mental hospital, as indeed it has, in some cases. The ideal for any religious community is that it be "a true family gathered together in the Lord's name and rejoicing in his presence (cf. Mt 18:20). . . . Brotherly unity shows that Christ has come (cf. Jn 13:35; 17:21); from it results great apostolic influence" (*Perfectae Caritatis* #15).

The continuation of the Prologue reiterates points already made: living "the word of life" (that is, the gospel), in the present moment and the presence of God; speaking the truth honestly, with charity to one's neighbor:

> Having our loins girded, therefore, with faith and the perform-
> ance of good works, let us walk in his paths by the guidance of the
> gospel, that we may deserve to see him who has called us to his
> kingdom. For if we wish to dwell in the tent of that kingdom, we
> must run to it by good deeds or we shall never reach it.
>
> But let us ask the Lord, with the prophet, "Lord, who shall dwell
> in your tent, or who shall rest upon your holy mountain?" After this
> question, brethren, let us listen to the Lord as he answers and shows
> us the way to that tent, saying, "He who walks without stain and
> practices justice; he who speaks the truth from his heart; he who has
> not used his tongue for deceit; he who has done no evil to his
> neighbor; he who has given no place to slander against his neigh-
> bor." (*Rule,* Prol.)

There are other ways of doing evil to our neighbor besides material theft or physical violence, as Benedict implies in adding the warning of Psalm 14/15 against slander. In any community one can create a hostile atmosphere of coldness, mistrust, indifference or contempt that can really hurt other individuals. This can be done by spreading slander about them, or creating cliques (an "in-group"), letting others know they are not included. Benedict is concerned that everyone feel that "we are all one in Christ," and no one is excluded. Creating such a spirit keeps us out of union with Christ, fit only to be cast into the fire (cf. Jn 15:6), unfit to "dwell in his tent or rest upon his holy mountain"; Christ will not accept the gift, at the altar, of one who is divided from his brother (cf. Mt 5:23). The spiritual combat is carried on in one's mind; the soul's enemies are primarily its thoughts, often stimulated by evil spirits:

> It is he who, under any temptation from the malicious devil, has brought him to naught by casting him and his temptation from the sight of his heart; and who has laid hold of his thoughts while they were still young and dashed them against Christ [cf. Ps 137:9].
>
> It is they who, fearing the Lord, do not pride themselves on their good observance; but, convinced that the good which is in them cannot come from themselves and must be from the Lord, glorify the Lord's work in them. . . .
>
> Hence the Lord says in the gospel, "Whoever listens to these words of mine and acts upon them, I will liken him to a wise man who built his house on a rock. The floods came, the winds blew and beat against that house, and it did not fall, because it was founded on rock."
>
> Having given us these assurances, the Lord is waiting every day for us to respond by our deeds to his holy admonitions. And the days of this life are lengthened and a truce granted us for this very reason, that we may amend our evil ways. As the apostle says, "Do you not know that God's patience is inviting you to repent?" For the merciful Lord tells us, "I desire not the death of the sinner, but that he should be converted and live." (*Rule,* Prol.)

This text reminds one of Mother Teresa of Calcutta's reply, when asked: why does God permit natural disasters, like tidal waves, floods, and hurricanes, to cause more loss of life among the poor than usually among the rich? She replied that God knows the poor are better prepared to enter eternal life.

> Therefore we must prepare our hearts and our bodies to do battle under the holy obedience of his commands, and let us ask God that he be pleased to give us the help of his grace for anything which our nature finds hardly possible. And if we want to escape the pains of hell and attain life everlasting, then, while there is still time, while we are still in the body and are able to fulfil all these things by the

light of this life, we must hasten to do now what will profit us for eternity.

And so we are going to establish a school of the Lord's way of service.[1] In founding it we hope to introduce nothing harsh or burdensome. But if a certain strictness results from the dictates of equity for the amendment of vices or the preservation of charity, do not be at once dismayed and fly from the way of salvation, whose entrance cannot but be narrow. For as we advance in the religious life and in faith, our hearts expand and we run the way of God's commandments with unspeakable sweetness of love. Thus, never departing from his school, but persevering in the monastery according to his teaching until death, we may by patience share in the sufferings of Christ and deserve to have a share also in his kingdom. (*Rule*, Prol.)

Notice how often Benedict says "we must run," "we must hasten. . . ." The time is short.

There is a danger that the routine of a "school of the Lord's way of service" may turn into just a succession of monotonous acts. So much so, that for some souls such an ordered life is not a suitable way to do God's will; that is why there is a year's novitiate, in which to test it before committing oneself forever. But even in such a well-regulated routine the will of God will surprise us in unforeseen ways and perhaps turn our plans and expectations upside down. This overturning of our plans and of our own will, leads to temptations to give up. (G. K. Chesterton commented once that "Christianity has been tried, and found difficult.")

In the phrase "by patience to share in the sufferings of Christ" there is a play on words, "patience" and "suffering" having the same root in Latin. Benedict is encouraging us to believe we are on the right road toward the fulfillment of human nature's ultimate desire to see God, if we experience something like a share in Christ's feelings of abandonment on the cross. Paradoxically, there is "cause for rejoicing" if "for a time you have to suffer the distress of many trials" (1 Pt 1:6).

---

1. In the past, this has been translated as "a school of the Lord's service." But many scholars are agreed that a more accurate translation is "the Lord's *way of service*." There is a significant difference, between a school which teaches how to serve the Lord, and a school which teaches the Lord's way of serving both God and human beings. It hinges on how to translate the Latin adjective *dominici*.

The Prologue is an echo of the preaching of John the Baptist, a call to conversion, inviting us to listen to the voice of God and incline our will to his, in order to reach our unique place in God's eternal scheme of things. Seek peace and quiet; be much more of a listener than a talker; listen with reverence; if you must speak, speak the truth from your heart. In other words, walk in the presence of God under the guidance of the gospel, in order to deserve to see him who has called us to his kingdom. To start with, ask God for the help of his grace; then never give up; be assured that eventually you will arrive at the love of God, as close as possible to the paradise of intimacy with him enjoyed by Adam and Eve before their fall.

Humility, the First Four Degrees

Chapter 7 of the Rule of Benedict, "On Humility," is the heart of Benedict's teaching and can be particularly helpful to us for arriving in practice at real Christian love—"the pursuit of perfect charity following the teaching and example of the Divine Master" being the essence of religious life (cf. *Perfectae Caritatis* #1). The Rule of Benedict is written for those of us who do not yet know the true meaning of love, the virtue which reassumes all others, assimilates us to Christ, and is our final goal. As an example (a true story) of what we mean by the *wrong* idea, when asked why her husband was seeking to have her murdered, the reason a young mother gave was: "Because he loves me." His love was of the possessive kind, which would not tolerate her having any independence by taking a job (night duty as a registered nurse); he wanted complete control over her—all or nothing. This is very different from the unselfish love which wants not one's own will for others but God's, so that they may live as freely and as happily as possible. This kind of love is a deliberate act of the will, which gives rather than takes. We can come to it through the practice of what we can understand: humility. (At least, that is what Benedict believed, as is clear from the last sentences of the Prologue, as well as from chapter 7 of the Rule.)

"Love" and "charity" are the words we use, to try to translate into English the original Greek New Testament word *agape*. But in common usage they have come to have a somewhat different meaning. The result has been, in practice, that well-meaning individuals, aiming at a life of Christian perfection, have committed blunders in the name of "love," of which they have an imperfect notion—imperfect because not detached from selfishness or possessiveness: from pride, if you like; or else because they identify it solely with an emotion, or confuse it with "almsgiving," in the sense of "Catholic charities," which is indeed one of the potential expressions of charity but not the whole thing. To give to the poor, expecting nothing for oneself in return, to endow schools and hospitals or give volunteer service to the sick, are acts of love in the Christian sense because they imitate and, as it were, reincarnate the love with which God the Son assumed a human life and gave all of it for us (who are very poor and sick in the spiritual sense), even to the shedding of his blood. A Baptist preacher once said that how much you give does not count so much (as an act of Christian charity) as how little you have left afterwards. For some people to give ten dollars may mean to go without a meal; to do this gladly for the love of God, because in the poor we see the face of Christ, without taking pride in it like the Pharisee in the Temple[1] is truly charity. Our imperfection gave rise to the phrase "As cold as charity," referring to the way we show our "charitableness" sometimes, in speech or deeds. True charity comes from the warm heart of Christ.

Holy scripture, brethren, cries out to us, saying, "Everyone who exalts himself shall be humbled, and he who humbles himself shall be exalted. . . ." Hence, if we wish to reach the very highest point of humility and to arrive speedily at that heavenly exaltation to which ascent is made through the humility of this present life, we must by our ascending actions erect the ladder Jacob saw in his dream, on which angels appeared to him descending and ascending. By that descent and ascent we must surely understand nothing else than this, that we descend by self-exaltation and ascend by humility. And the ladder thus set up is our life in the world, which the Lord raises up to heaven if our heart is humbled. For we call our body and soul the sides of the ladder, and into these sides our divine vocation has inserted the different steps of humility and discipline we must climb. (*Rule* 7)

Benedict's poetic application of Jacob's dream at Bethel (Gn 28:12) to the spiritual life is certainly not to be taken as a piece of "critical exegesis" (the modern method for arriving at exactly what an author had in mind, the literal sense of scripture); his way of using sacred scripture deserves a long

---

1. Jesus spoke this parable addressed to those who believed in their own self-righteousness while holding everyone else in contempt: "Two men went up to the temple to pray; one was a Pharisee, the other a tax collector. The Pharisee with head unbowed prayed in this fashion: 'I give thanks, O God, that I am not like the rest of men. . . . I fast twice a week. I pay tithes on all I possess [give ten percent to charity].' The other man, however, kept his distance, not even daring to raise his eyes to heaven. All he did was beat his breast and say, 'O God, be merciful to me, a sinner.' Believe me, this man went home from the temple justified but the other did not. For everyone who exalts himself shall be humbled while he who humbles himself shall be exalted" (Lk 18:9-14).

painstaking article; suffice it here to say that as a method of teaching, it gets its point across by good use of the imagination.

> The first degree [or step] of humility, then, is that a person keep the fear of God before his eyes and beware of ever forgetting it. Let him be ever mindful of all that God has commanded and constantly turn over in his heart how hell will burn for their sins those who despise God; and how eternal life has been prepared for those that fear him. Let him be on his guard at every moment against sins and vices, whether of the mind, the tongue, the hands, the feet, or self-will, and also against the desires of the flesh. (*Rule* 7)

Sin is always an act solely of the will, in violation of one's conscience; it is more or less rhetorical to add the mind, natural desires, and physical organs, as if they could be sinful of themselves. Their mention is an aid to the examination of conscience, because it is in their mis-use that the will can sin. "Self-will" does not mean, of course, the power of choice, God's gift which makes us free and distinguishes us from lower animals. It stands for selfishness, making choices without regard to what other people have a right to expect, or in opposition to those rights, and in contradiction to God's commandments and his design for us. We are the work of art, he is the artist. Cooperate with him by using the power of choice responsibly, recognizing your responsibilities to your Creator and to your fellow beings—and ultimately to your true self.

Sins of the mind: watch what you think about. Beware also of intellectual pride; hang on to the faith known only to the simple and the humble, which is taught by the See of Peter.

Of the tongue: be careful that what you say is appropriate and true.

Of the hands: watch what you touch, and what you take (that it does not belong to somebody else), and avoid physical violence.

Of the feet: don't let them carry you where you don't belong.

We may note here another of Benedict's frequent appeals to human nature's natural desire of God ("eternal life"), which he wishes us to satisfy, using the gospel and the Rule as our guide.

> Let a man consider that God is always looking at him from heaven, that his actions are everywhere visible to the divine eyes and are constantly being reported to God by the angels. This is what the prophet shows us when he represents God as ever present within

our thoughts, in the words "Searcher of minds and hearts is God" and again in the words "The Lord knows the thoughts of men." Again he says, "You have read my thoughts from afar" and "The thoughts of men will confess to you." In order that he may be careful about his wrongful thoughts, therefore, let the faithful brother say constantly in his heart, "Then shall I be spotless before him, if I have kept myself from my iniquity."

As for self-will, we are forbidden to do our own will by the scripture, which says to us, "Turn away from your own will," and likewise by the prayer in which we ask God that his will be done in us. And rightly are we taught not to do our own will, when we take heed to the warning of scripture: "There are ways which to men seem right, but the ends of them plunge into the depths of hell"; and also when we tremble at what is said of the careless: "They are corrupt and have become abominable in their wills."

And as for the desires of the flesh, let us believe with the prophet that God is ever present to us, when he says to the Lord, "Every desire of mine is before you." We must be on our guard, therefore, against evil desires, for death lies close by the gate of pleasure. Hence the scripture gives this command: "Pursue not your lusts." (*Rule* 7)

Taken by itself, the paragraph just quoted might strike the reader as too puritanical. Benedict's true meaning is well interpreted by the following notes from remarks made on the virtue of temperance by Dom Leonce Crenier, at a retreat given at Portsmouth Priory, Rhode Island, before he went to found a monastery in Martinique in 1947, after many years as superior of Saint Benoit du Lac in Quebec. "Pleasure is not to be indulged in indiscriminately. Some people's lives are just one pleasure after another. . . . Pleasure is attached to certain obligatory actions in order to help us to perform them. But those actions are not to be performed more than is necessary, so that they are being done solely for pleasure, all need having been exhausted. But we can enjoy them up to that point. The marital act may be performed not only for procreation but also to increase and renew conjugal love: but not just for pleasure. A man cannot live long without any pleasure. If he has no spiritual pleasure, he will turn to carnal. And he needs, too, a little physical pleasure: if not what is licit and good, then he'll take what's illicit and evil."

So therefore, since the eyes of the Lord observe the good and the evil and the Lord is always looking down from heaven on the children of men "to see if there be anyone who understands and seeks God"[1] and since our deeds are daily, day and night, reported to the Lord by the angels assigned to us, we must constantly beware, brethren, as the prophet says in the psalm, lest at any time God see us falling into evil ways and becoming unprofitable; and lest, having spared us for the present because in his kindness he awaits our reformation, he say to us in the future, "These things you did, and I held my peace."

The second degree of humility is that a person love not his own will nor take pleasure in satisfying his desires, but model his actions on the saying of the Lord, "I have come not to do my own will, but the will of him who sent me." It is written also, "Self-will has its punishment, but subjection wins a crown."

The third degree of humility is that a person for love of God submit himself to his superior in all obedience, imitating the Lord, of whom the apostle says, "He became obedient even unto death." (*Rule* 7)

Individuals have entered monastic life not with the intention of remaining a simple monk, "obedient even unto death," but of becoming an abbot, or rising to some other position of authority within the monastery, or even outside it; or else hoping to find it a quiet place, where they will be supported and left alone to pursue their independent interests, perhaps to become a famous theologian or artist. This is not only contrary to the virtue of humility but leads to "the evil zeal of bitterness" (cf. *Rule* 72)—part of self-will's punishment, when their ambition is unfulfilled.[2]

---

1. It is significant that right choices also depend on *understanding* who God is and what his will is; Jesus often rebuked his critics and not infrequently the apostles themselves, for their lack of understanding.
2. Their frustration has been expressed in these simple verses:
   I saw a man who put his hope in power and success,
   his jowls hung down, his back was bent,
   sad his shifty eyes, and black his dress.
   Hopeful friends came to him, and went.
   The morning sun of childhood gave way to night,
   the nothingness of lack of light.
   He studied suffering for love,
   but could not pass the test.

The arrival at such honors is not a bad thing, if it is God's will rather than the satisfaction of the person's desires. Of itself it does not necessarily bring us closer to God, which is the great ambition of the humble. Benedictines have contributed much to the Church and to humanity as popes and bishops as well as by being abbots and have done so with no loss of humility, especially when they would have preferred, if it were up to them, to "win the crown" of remaining "in subjection." The fact that they had loved living in subjection made them all the better at exercising authority. Those who contributed so much to liturgical music, did so largely anonymously; likewise the illuminators of manuscripts and the builders or decorators of churches. Benedict has a whole chapter "On the Craftsmen of the Monastery"; he does not discourage the practice of the arts or the development of talent, provided it is done in obedience and humility. The humble artist knows realistically that his talent is a gift of God, over which he must not be proud but responsible and grateful. A text of the Prologue which we have left till now says: "Convinced that the good which is in them cannot come from themselves and must be from the Lord, they glorify the Lord's work in them, using the words of the prophet, 'Not to us, O Lord, not to us, but to your name give the glory.' Thus also the apostle Paul attributed nothing of the success of his preaching to himself but said, 'By the grace of God I am what I am.' And again he says, 'He who glories, let him glory in the Lord.' "To the preaching and writing of Paul we may compare the missionaries that have lived the Benedictine Rule, and spiritual writers, several of the greatest having been nuns—Saint Gertrude, for instance, a German contemporary of the poet Dante, and Saint Hildegarde of Bingen (1098-1179), another German, in whom there is renewed interest today; she was also a musician. It was by no lack of humility that they wrote or spoke as well as they could, to try to be worthy of their subject.

> If there are craftsmen in the monastery, let them practice their crafts with all humility, provided the abbot has given permission. But if any one of them becomes conceited over his skill in his craft, because he seems to be conferring a benefit on the monastery [there is no "indispensable man"], let him be taken from his craft and no longer exercise it unless, after he has humbled himself, the abbot again gives him permission. (*Rule* 57)

Given the choice, Benedict would rather give the world another humble saint than a great artist. It is unwise to think of our talents with self-conceit, or of ourselves or anybody else as indispensable; it smacks of idolatry. Benedict is pointing to a truth which does not apply to monastics alone; here his Rule is illustrating how a monastery can be a microcosm of the world.

Benedict is not denying that our talents, our very existence, are a benefit to the human race and its environment; he is only affirming that they are God's gift, and it would be better that they be taken away, if otherwise you, or some other person, would take such pride in them that their glory would not be ascribed rightfully to God, without whom we can do nothing. There is truth in saying that everyone is irreplaceable; no one else can be what you are, or what you are meant to be, even though you may be only like a small stone in the great mosaic of the universe. No one else can do exactly what you can do, and you have only your own lifetime in which to do it. (So #47 of the Instruments of Good Works advises us "To keep death daily before one's eyes" [*Rule* 4]). You are irreplaceable but not indispensable, which means God is able to fulfill his plan for the world without your help, if need be. Jesus Christ is the one and only exception to that rule.

To illustrate what Benedict means, we may use the example of a Benedictine who was a famous organist and liturgist; he was so afraid that his music would take the place of prayer in his life, that he gave it up, except for organ accompaniment of the monastic choir. He would still compose new music for a Mass, on request—he could finish it in a day; but to occupy his free time, he replaced music with New Testament studies, until he died in 1992 in his late eighties. Many then wondered if anyone else, out of about thirty monks, could be found capable of replacing him at the organ. No less than five came forward, out of God's providence, and were assigned to do it in rotation. There will never be another Dom Gregory Murray; but God wanted that community's model liturgy to survive and was at no loss to provide for it.

In civil life, Americans wondered if a replacement could be found for a president of the stature of Roosevelt, whom they had elected to four terms. When mortality caught up with him, most wondered who this Harry Truman was. Truman himself said there were a million Americans who could hold the post just as well as he (all Democrats, one infers from other statements of his!); if there was an element of greatness in him, humility was part of it. A generation later, estimable historians could dispute which was the greater, he or Roosevelt.

And in the Church, there have been few men in the papacy as brilliant as

Pius XII; older Catholics can remember that one could not imagine the Church without him. Hardly anyone had heard of Angelo Roncalli, seventy-eight years old when he was elected to succeed Pius XII; even his sister said, "*What?* little Angelo!?!" But he no sooner appeared as John XXIII, than he conquered the heart of the whole world and brought about abiding changes far beyond ecclesiastical circles, not expected from a supposedly conservative institution. Pius XII was almost forgotten, which was not entirely fair, since his writings were the basis of the decrees of Vatican II no less than the writings of the Fathers of the Church.

So if you feel like a Roosevelt or a Pius XII in your own vocation, Benedict would have you give the glory to God, and perhaps to someone—your wife or husband, or a whole community or team without whose help you could not achieve so much. And remember God may be planning to replace you, with a Truman or a John XXIII.

Admittedly, there are mysteries about God's plans. Nations and cultures fall into decline; so do monasteries, sometimes at the loss of saintly abbots; and Catholic theology has had its not so golden ages, though the Church as a whole has never been without saints of some kind. God will never abandon his Church, nor anyone else unless they abandon him. A Shakespeare, a Michelangelo, or a Beethoven have hardly been succeeded by equals; but their works outlive them, so a successor is not needed, and the same is true in the Church—writings like those of Benedict or Augustine need no replacement, just commentary and interpretation, in order to be better understood or relevant when times have changed.

> If any of the work of the craftsmen is to be sold, let those through whose hands the transactions pass see to it that they do not presume to practice any fraud. . . . And in the prices let not the sin of avarice creep in, but let the goods always be sold a little cheaper than they can be sold by people in the world, "that in all things God may be glorified."[1]

The fourth degree of humility is that he hold fast to patience with a silent mind when in this obedience he meets with difficulties and contradictions and even any kind of injustice, enduring all without growing weary or running away. For scripture says, "He who

---

1. Benedict's motivation for lowering prices is not to engage in "price wars," but to edify the world by avoiding even the appearance of greed.

perseveres to the end, he it is who shall be saved"; and again, "Let your heart take courage, and wait for the Lord!" And to show how those who are faithful ought to endure all things, however contrary, for the Lord, the scripture says in the person of the suffering, "For your sake we are put to death all the day long; we are considered as sheep marked for slaughter." Then, secure in their hope of a divine recompense, they go on with joy to declare, "But in all these trials we conquer, through him who has granted us his love." Again, in another place scripture says, "You have tested us, O God; you have tried us as silver is tried, by fire; you have brought us into a snare; you have laid afflictions on our back." And to show that we ought to be under a superior, it goes on to say, "You have set men over our heads."

Moreover, by their patience those faithful ones fulfill the Lord's command in adversities and injuries: when struck on one cheek, they offer the other; when deprived of their tunic, they surrender also their cloak; when forced to go a mile, they go two; with the apostle Paul they bear with false brethren and bless those who curse them. (*Rule* 7)

Many who know how unfair life can be, consider this Fourth Degree of Humility and chapter 68 (which we shall quote below) to be the most beautiful passages of the Rule, comparing them to the legendary discourse "On Perfect Joy" in "The Little Flowers of Saint Francis." "Hold fast to patience with a silent mind," not letting your joy grow sour by brooding over life's hurts. One is reminded of some of the Instruments of Good Works: Not to nurse a grudge. Not a grumbler. To do no wrong to anyone, and to bear patiently wrongs done to oneself (*Rule* 4). Why let them get you down, when you can use them to climb higher on the ladder? But the injured party will reveal any natural feelings of anger or depression about them to his abbot or another counselor: "When evil thoughts come into one's heart, to dash them against Christ immediately. And to manifest them to one's spiritual father" (*Rule* 4).

The "difficulties, contradictions, and injustices" Benedict expects a monk may suffer are not necessarily caused by malice on the part of superiors. Is it not common experience that those by whom we get hurt the most are often those by whom we are loved the most, and that we ourselves accidentally hurt those we love, as we can see in hindsight, when all we wanted to do was help, and we tried our best to avoid hurting them? If a gifted child is sent away to school, to the parents it feels like a sacrifice made for the sake of giving their child the best possible education; but to the child it may feel like rejection. Abbots have been known to suffer deeply, because what they intended as help to one of their monks turned out to be detrimental or was misunderstood as malicious. One way to avoid hurting others or making mistakes is to do nothing, except that this too would often be a mistake, felt as a sign of "neglect, or undervaluing the welfare of the souls committed to [the abbot]" (*Rule* 2).

A familiar sort of contradiction which feels like injustice is suffered by the young adult whose engagement is opposed and even "broken up" by parents who foresee that a marriage he or she wishes to make could not turn out happily, not perhaps because of the character of the person their child loves, but because of the in-laws involved. Young people often do not realize that one marries, so to speak, into one's spouse's whole family. There are reasons for believing that "arranged marriages" worked out, percentage-wise, better than "love matches," because married life is difficult, and its difficulties may be anticipated and coped with better, when there is less emotion involved. Likewise a superior may have to veto some project on which a monk has set his heart, because he foresees insuperable difficulties. This is experienced by the monk as contradiction and even injustice. But in truth it is not necessarily brought about by any lack of trust, admiration, or love for him as a person. However we may be fortunate in today's tendency to allow the young more freedom than was often the case in the past, to take responsibility for their lives once they have reached a certain degree of maturity. Experience is a good teacher, and people can be trusted to learn from their mistakes. Attempts of parents or religious superiors to control every aspect of their dependents' lives is seen as unacceptable interference hindering their development. But this principle too can be pushed too far, leading to permissiveness: an excess of freedom. The senior person some-times has to interfere, otherwise the junior will be justified in asking, "Why didn't you tell me?" In either case, Benedict advises that the "victims" suffer patiently "with a silent mind," that is, not brooding over their hurt, complain-ing, or assuming ill-will or lack of understanding in the superior or parent.

There is said to have been an abbot who would call in his novices and ask them what they would really like to do. Then he would assign them the opposite. Not out of malice or some kind of spiritual sadism, but because he believed this policy would strengthen the novice's virtues of humility and obedience, precisely by testing them. But it could break them. For instance, if the subject wanted to study theology, he might be sent to get a degree in the natural sciences, or vice versa. If he loved the idea of going onto the community's foreign missions, he might be put in charge of building maintenance, or the printing press, or some department of agriculture, practiced at the home monastery. The abbot believed the sacrifice of native talent or interest was worth the added merit of humility and obedience. This came to be perceived as inhuman, unwise and inefficient (and certainly not funny), because we generally do not do anything so well as that for which we have native talent or about which we feel enthusiastic. But it is the kind of thing that happens everywhere in life, not just in monasteries nor usually by anyone's choice, that a square peg is put into a round hole and a key into a lock not made for it. Benedict was aware that it happens, but he does not advocate it: "Let the house of God be managed by prudent men and in a prudent manner," he writes elsewhere (*Rule* 53), "that no one may be troubled or vexed in the house of God" (*Rule* 31). Nevertheless, since we are going to meet with trouble and vexation and stupidity, he tells us a technique for making the best of it.

A monk has no rights, according to a few monastic theorists. Benedict was of a different mind, or he would not speak of "injustices." No less than any other human being, a monk or nun needs a minimum amount of food (for both body and soul), sleep, and clothing. Benedict provides for all of these; for example, a substantial amount of time for daily spiritual reading, one or two meals a day, roughly seven hours sleep at night, and an afternoon siesta according to Mediterranean custom, and different clothing for summer and winter.

"Work and pray" is a motto ascribed to the Benedictines, though not found in the Rule; but it happens that more of one or the other gets imposed in (as well as outside) monasteries, than Benedict prescribes. For instance, a Jesuit said—in amazement—that in his society the jobs held by a certain Benedictine would be distributed between five or six men. "The trouble today is that monks live too long," said that Benedictine's abbot, when the subject's doctor found him to be close to critical condition from sheer exhaustion and prescribed six months total rest at once. The abbot did not mean to say, "I wish you were dead." He just longed for "the good old days" when, for instance at the Canterbury monastery in the fifteenth century, few monks lived beyond their forties. This monk was in his fifties. For the good of the community, he had to try to continue on the job for another year. He obeyed and lived to go to Lourdes and also get the aforesaid six months rest. Foreseeing such problems, Benedict wrote chapter 68, "If a Brother Is Commanded to Do Impossible Things":

> If it happens that difficult or impossible tasks are laid on a brother, let him nevertheless receive the order of the one in authority with all meekness and obedience. But if he sees that the weight of the burden altogether exceeds the limit of his strength, let him submit the reasons for his inability to the one who is over him in a quiet way and at an opportune time, without pride, resistance, or contradiction. And if after these representations the superior still persists in his decision and command, let the subject know that this is for his good, and let him obey out of love, trusting in the help of God.

In the example given, help came all right.

The submission of protest "in a quiet way and at an opportune time, without pride, resistance, or contradiction" is reminiscent of "holding fast to patience with a silent mind." Benedict prescribes faith, hope, and charity as a simple way for a humble person to cope, if the superior persists in his decision and command: with faith that obedience is for his own good, with hope in God's help, and out of love for God and God's will. And this is in the spirit of Paul's First Letter to the Corinthians: "Now there remain faith, hope, and love, these three, but the greatest of these is love. Love is patient, is kind. . . . Love is not proud, does not seek what is its own, is not vexed. . . . It believes all things, hopes all things, endures all things. Love never falls away" (13:13, 4-8). Today people might think of getting a lawyer. Do not imagine that Benedict never thought of that, since in chapter 3 he says, "Let no one in the monastery presume to contend with his abbot in an insolent way or even outside of the monastery."

We said above that the suffering which Benedict foresaw as possibly befalling a monk (and he had probably seen or heard of real cases) is not necessarily caused by malice or ill-will on the part of superiors. Far from it. Is it however conceivable, either to us or to Benedict himself, that even a Benedictine abbot could be guilty of malice, ill-will, or neglect of his subjects' good? Of course it is. All humans are subject to human weakness, and superiors (people with power over others and responsibility for a community or corporation) are subject to particular temptations, as a sort of occupational hazard. Benedict has already mentioned some of them: favoritism and greater concern for material things than for the welfare of souls. While preaching to others, an abbot may become reprobate, if he does not watch out for his own soul and, by good and holy deeds, live up to his title as the one who acts in the place of Christ in the monastery, displaying the affection of a father, as a shepherd and a physician of souls (cf. *Rule* 2). Another danger, mentioned in chapter 65, "On the Prior of the Monastery," is envy. (The prior is a sort of second in command after the abbot, a kind of vice president or lieutenant governor; Benedict seems to have had trouble with at least one of them and advises the appointment of several deans to share in the governance of a community, rather than the appointment of just one.) Having painted an almost livid portrait of how a prior could undermine the brethren's unity and peace, to such a point that he ought to be expelled from the monastery, Benedict concludes the chapter with a caution, harking back to the theme of the judgment we will have to face: "But the abbot should bear in mind that he will have to render an account to God for all his judgments, lest the flame of envy or jealousy be kindled in his soul."

No spirituality would be complete or adequate, without giving us guidance on how to deal in a Christian spirit, not only with our own sins, but with the sins of others which may affect us. The way Jesus underwent his passion is Benedict's model and motive for suffering other people's ill-will, and we must remind ourselves that, at least according to Benedict, it is not other people but our own self-will and pride that is the chief enemy to overcome.

Someone may be the undeserving object of another's envy. Benedict suggests the example of a prior. He is aware of priors who think of themselves as second abbots, then as rival abbots, currying favor with disgruntled or rebellious brothers in order to get themselves made the one and only abbot; it sometimes happens that they bring about their abbot's deposition or resignation but fail to get elected in his place, and even lose the post of prior, which serves them right.

But it can also happen that the prior, or another of the monks, innocently acquires the graces and virtues expected of an abbot, with the result that many of his brethren turn to him as a sort of guru, just as good as the abbot himself, and even better than he as a counselor or physician of their souls. He may be more embarrassed by this than his abbot; but what can he do? Certainly do all he can to strengthen the reverence they have for their superior, and their unity with him; and try to quell any tendency to "disorder, dissensions, rivalry, detraction, and quarrels" (*Rule* 65). As is clear from chapter 27, "How Solicitous the Abbot Should Be for the Excommunicated," the abbot ought to rely on having monks like these, who can help him solidify his monks' loyalty when it wavers or begins to dissolve. But he might feel unreasonably insecure and anxious about his own influence and authority, and actually do both the community and the prior (or whoever it may be) an injustice by finding some way of expelling him.

We mentioned above the case of a husband who was so possessive, so determined to control every moment of his wife's life, that when he failed he sought to have her murdered. Jealousy, envy and suspicion can lead to extremes. In human relations, in every kind of society, including families and monasteries, true love gives trust and does not withdraw or invade another's legitimate freedom. As we have seen in chapter 64, the abbot must "not be excitable and worried, nor exacting and headstrong, nor jealous and over-suspicious; for then he is never at rest."

Another way envy may be detrimental to a community's best interests and lead to injustice to an individual, could be the acceptance into the monastery of a young man who proves to be popular with his peers and intellectually very gifted. The superiors (the abbot and his aides, the lesser superiors) may refuse to let him do the studies required for ordination to the priesthood, because then he would be eligible for the Abbacy, thus a threat to the superior's power (today, only a priest may be made an abbot, though in Benedict's time, it was not a clerical post). If he has not a college degree already, they might not let him get one, so that he would not be eligible to become a department head, or the principal, president, or rector, replacing those who hold such positions, should the work of the monastery include conducting a college, high school, or seminary. Should he get a degree in economics or business administration, he might be seen as a threat to whoever holds the post of Cellarer (about whom, more later). This repressing of talent might not be motivated by envy but by mistrust of his loyalty, the fear that higher education would tempt him to accept offers of prestigious and remu-nerative posts elsewhere, as indeed has happened in the case of more than one religious. Should such a young man be deprived of higher education, for these or any other reasons, if he is humble he can become the type we described before as a "box of spare parts," the one and only type Benedict permits the abbot to love more than others. But the community has lost the benefits that might have come from his further education.

In any case, it is perfectly clear what the sufferer must do, if he is to climb the fourth step, or degree, of humility. He is "to obey in all things the commands of the abbot, even though the abbot himself (which God forbid) should act otherwise, mindful of the Lord's precept, 'Do what they say, but not what they do' " (#60 of the Instruments of Good Works, *Rule* 4).

It is hard to do, but persevere, says Benedict, "enduring all without growing weary or running away." If you feel you cannot go on, "wait for the Lord": for his help now, and his eternal recompense later—the virtue of hope. "To desire eternal life with all the passion of the spirit. To put one's hope in God. And never to despair of God's mercy," are other Instruments of Good Works. All this is "for the Lord. Preferring nothing to the love of Christ" (*Rule* 4), not even the trust and respect of one's superiors, "they go on with joy," always embracing the cross and the Crucified as soon as he presents himself, with the energy provided by "him who has granted us his love." "You have brought us into a snare," says the psalmist, who felt trapped. Why should a lover of Christ not have his fidelity put to such tests, when the Lord himself suffered no less and people in the world of unbelievers suffer the same sort of ways? The Fathers of the Second Vatican Council could have intended to remind Benedictines of this passage of the Rule, when they wrote: "Those who profess the evangelical counsels love and seek *before all else* that God who took the initiative in loving us (cf. 1 Jn 4:10)."

Benedict reminds us that our Lord told us to expect such trials and how to overcome them; and he gave us the example of Paul, who bore with false brethren, the sort that fail to live up to these Instruments of Good Works: "Not to entertain deceit in one's heart. Not to give a false peace. Not to forsake charity." Praying the psalms, the monk may have to apply what is said of "enemies" to his own brethren, practicing the Instruments: "Not to curse those who curse us, but rather to bless them. To bear persecution for justice' sake. To pray for one's enemies in the love of Christ." But always bear in mind that your worst enemy is your own pride; overcome that, and you will have overcome all the others. (But in *Mere Christianity*, C. S. Lewis warns us that if we think we are free from it, then we are not.) It is like a beard that has to be shaved every day, a weed that grows in all climates and all seasons.

Although the word "men," in the verse, "You have set men over our heads" is *homines* in Latin, meaning "human beings" in general, not only "males," it may call to mind the injuries suffered by "battered women," a very grave moral problem and all too common in our society. Since our presentation of Benedict's spirituality is intended to be helpful also to the laity, more than half of whom are women and many of them married, it would be insensitive and unworthy of Benedict's realism not to ask how this degree of humility applies to them. Once the wedding is over, and they have entered their new home, alone with their husband and the door locked behind them, they do not know what they may be in for. It will not always be paradise, but not all will find themselves (thank God) "like sheep marked for slaughter."

Saint Benedict's Rule gives no guidelines explicitly for married life—of course. But we think some of his Instruments of Good Works apply, though they present a challenge no one could meet without the grace of God: "Not to forsake charity. Not to return evil for evil. Not to curse those who curse us, but rather to bless them. To pray for one's enemies in the love of Christ. To love one's enemies." Sadly, the beloved spouse can turn into a dangerous enemy. But: "To do no wrong to anyone, and to bear patiently wrongs done to oneself" needs some qualification. "Thou shalt not kill" also means that we must not allow either others or oneself to be killed, or maimed, if we can prevent it; and it is not only her own life that a married woman must defend but also, if she is pregnant, her child's. Therefore: "Not to do to another what one would not have done to oneself" (the "golden rule") applies: do not let your child's life go undefended. We think that: "To help in trouble" also can be interpreted: "To get help in trouble." And: "To manifest [evils] to one's spiritual father" can imply manifesting them to a marriage counselor. True love for one's neighbor does not require sweeping his sins under the carpet but helping him overcome them for the future, as if they were one's own. Saint Margaret of Scotland suffered much injustice of another kind from her husband, but she bore it patiently and with love for him, expressed in converting him gradually from his weaknesses, getting him to reform.

Except for cases like this, humility is very simple but impossibly hard without grace. If we thought it impossible but got to know people who had reached this degree of humility, it would be equally impossible not to love what we saw, envy them and admire them. They have really achieved freedom and the greatest of triumphs.

Humility, the Last Eight Degrees

> The fifth degree of humility is that he hide from his abbot none of the evil thoughts that enter his heart or the sins committed in secret, but that he humbly confess them. The scripture urges us to this when it says, "Reveal your way to the Lord and hope in him," and again, "Confess to the Lord, for he is good, for his mercy endures forever." And the prophet likewise says, "My offense I have made known to you, and my iniquities I have not covered up. I said: 'I will declare against myself my iniquities to the Lord'; and 'You forgave the wickedness of my heart.'" (*Rule* 7)

This manifestation of the heart to a spiritual father was already an integral part of traditional monastic practice by Benedict's time. It is humiliating, if done honestly; but it is extremely helpful, even indispensable, for progress in the spiritual life and even for mental or emotional health, as has been rediscovered in modern times.

You may object that it can be overdone; individuals can become too dependent on their therapist or director and prudence is required in their selection. But an abbot worthy of his name is presumed by Benedict to have the necessary qualifications, which include being able to keep his advisers from becoming too dependent or not taking enough responsibility for their own decisions. The primary requirement for being a good counselor is being a good listener; the "client's" primary need is to get his thoughts and feelings honestly off his chest, to someone he can trust to keep them confidential. In chapter 46 "On Those Who Fail in Any Other Matters," that is, on the requirement of "making satisfaction" and confessing his fault, if anyone in the course of his work "has broken something or lost something, or transgresses in any other way whatsoever," Benedict adds: "But if the sin-sickness of the soul is a hidden one, let him reveal it only to the abbot or to a spiritual father, who knows how to cure his own and others' wounds without exposing them and making them public." This latter precaution is of the utmost importance; some people are "sieves" and gossips, who are just incapable of keeping private information to themselves, even when told about them in confession or in confidence. One has to beware against seeking counsel or making confessions to a person of that type. If the counselor or spiritual father is an experienced person, with common sense and a little patience and charity, it is not very hard to get good advice toward "curing our wounds."

The study of the spiritual life is the study of an art, not of a science, and to become a good practitioner of an art one needs teachers. Arts have their rules (with a scientific basis, to some extent), and artists must learn them; but good artists know also how and when to break them. Augustine Baker, a Benedictine wise in the spiritual life (and already mentioned above), cautions against too frequent confession and examination of conscience, advising the more positive approach of docility to the Holy Spirit, our principal teacher. Baker fears that otherwise one may become too self-absorbed and scrupulous. It is told of Saint Gertrude, for instance, that she was displeased one day at one of her sisters choosing not to receive communion. She asked in prayer, "Why, O merciful Lord, did you permit her to have that temptation?" He explained it was because the sister held the blanket of her unworthiness so close to her eyes, that she was not disposed to see the compassion in his paternal affection.

Note that Benedict advises the confession not only of deliberate sins but also of temptations: "evil thoughts that enter our hearts." (Two of the Instruments of Good Works are: "When evil thoughts come into one's heart, to dash them against Christ immediately. And to manifest them to one's spiritual father.") And he concludes with: "You forgave the wickedness of my heart." He advises us to face the fact of wickedness in our hearts (there is usually some even in the heart of a saint) and confess it, even though it has led to no conscious sin by consent of the will. He means sexual, angry, even murderous inclinations; gross ambition and vanity; grudges and resentment; suspicions, doubts, discouragement, depression. Our Lord spoke of the same: "What emerges from within a man, that and nothing else is what makes him impure. Wicked designs come from the deep recesses of the heart" (Mk 7:22-23). Besides the kind of inclinations we have already mentioned, Jesus includes: "Acts of theft, greed, maliciousness, deceit, envy, blasphemy, arrogance, an obtuse spirit. All these evils come from within and render a man impure."

Pride can blind us to our sins and to our sinful tendencies. Because of the subtle workings of human psychology, not to mention the soul's demonic enemies, the more virtues we acquire, the more susceptible we can be made to suppressing the evidence that we can do wrong; when things around us do go wrong, we may then forget that the blame may be at least partially our own.

A person once told by an admirer that he evidently saw every side of difficult questions or problems, actually believed thereafter that he could never be wrong; this was a big mistake and led to more. As in the intellectual sphere, so also in the spiritual, people who realize they have achieved a degree of excellence can believe they do not need, like ordinary mortals, to work hard at developing more; if they give in to that temptation in the spiritual life, they will most probably regress. That is presumably why Benedict puts this step as the fifth, since to have made the fourth is already to have risen pretty high. "Beware of the lead," was a wise tennis coach's slogan; and a great football coach told his team to play as if the score were "nothing to nothing," although they were leading by three touchdowns to none.[1] In reminding us of the verse of the psalms, "Reveal your way to the Lord," Benedict is implying the Lord will respond by revealing in what ways your way needs to change; and in case you are shocked, discouraged, or depressed by his revelation, "hope in him . . . for he is good, for his mercy endures forever." The last of the Instruments of Good Works is "Never to despair of God's mercy"; self-knowledge can indeed tempt one to despair of ever arriving at Christian perfection or even at salvation; but with the revelation of the ways we need to improve, which can induce tears of sorrow, often comes also a deeper understanding and sense of God's mercy, which induces tears of joy. It is a grace worth praying for.

When one has perhaps been in a monastery for several years, or been part of some other prestigious religious group, steps may have to be taken to counteract just the opposite of the temptation to despair: the temptation to take pride in one's good fortune and to steal for ourselves the honors that may have accrued to us, as if they were not all attributable to the workings of God's grace, belonging properly to him. Augustine prayed, "Lord, grant that I may know myself, and that I may know you." There is a tale from the life of Saint Margaret of Cortona which illustrates the point. (She was a thirteenth century Franciscan tertiary, a Mary Magdalen type of penitent.) The sensational nature of her act of humility is more Franciscan than Benedictine, but as Francis received his first church from the Benedictines,

---

1. The New Testament too draws parallels between athletics and the spiritual life: cf. 1 Cor 9:24; Heb 12:1—etymologically the word "ascetic" means "athlete."

he may not mind our taking one of his disciples as an illustration. Her biographer tells that one night Satan inspired her with obsessive thoughts about the fame she had acquired. She climbed to the terrace of her home and tearfully cried out, "Get up, citizens of Cortona, get up, I tell you, and lose no time in driving me far away from you with stones; because I am the sinner who has committed [sins] against God and against my neighbor. . . ." At the top of her voice she proceeded to confess every sin of her life. The story illustrates these Instruments of Good Works: "To attribute to God, and not to self, whatever good one sees in oneself. But to recognize always that the evil is one's own doing, and to impute it to oneself" (*Rule* 4). True humility does not consist in saying one has not accomplished any good, or denying every good deed that even we have done, but in giving the proper place to God (praising and thanking him for his grace) and to ourselves (confessing our own wickedness).

> The sixth degree of humility is that a monk be content with the poorest and worst of everything, and that in every occupation assigned him he consider himself a bad and worthless workman, saying with the prophet, "I am brought to nothing and I am without understanding; I have become as a beast of burden before you, and I am always with you." (*Rule* 7)

This step raises problems about the difference between humility and low self-esteem, which we will take up more extensively at the seventh degree. Benedict does not say the humble *want* "the poorest and worst of everything" (that might be from sick self-esteem, even a kind of exhibitionism; some people are *proud* of their threadbare, ragged clothing and their dilapidated car—symbols of poverty—and look *down* on the rich). Benedict says they are simply *content* with poverty, if that is the way they have to live. Their happiness is not so fragile as to depend on status symbols or always having top quality, nor on the reverse. People should have what they need; these principles are set out in concrete detail in chapter 55, "On the Clothes and Shoes of the Brethren":

> Let clothing be given to the brethren according to the nature of the place in which they dwell and its climate; for in cold regions more will be needed and in warm regions less. This is to be taken into consideration, therefore, by the abbot.

This sounds like common sense, and it is. But it is not always followed: for instance, in Captain Scott's expedition to the South Pole, the first ever made, as a matter of principle the explorers wore nothing but the regular uniform of the Royal Navy. It is not surprising that they did not survive. Religious orders as well as the military need to adapt their dress to the actual living conditions and to some extent to local custom.

Benedict goes on to say that the monk's dress must be "sufficient" and specifies what articles are to be recommended, including stockings and shoes. "The monks must not complain about the color or coarseness of any of these things but be content with what can be found in the district where they live and can be purchased cheaply." So it does not have to be "the poorest and worst" available. "The abbot shall see to the size of the garments, that they be not too short for those who wear them but of the proper fit." Christians should not give the Church a bad name by dressing in ways that look ridiculous, for instance in clothes that do not fit; neither do they have to punish or annoy themselves with clothing that is deliberately made uncomfortable. The abbot should show the same concern for his monks' dress as a good mother would for her children.

"Let those who receive new clothes always give back the old ones at once, to be put away in the wardrobe for the poor." So Benedict would have even monks dress better than the poor, though they must not give in to discontent if only "the poorest and worst" of clothing is available. "Any superfluity in clothing should be taken away. Those who are sent on a journey should receive new underclothing, which they are to wash and give back when they return. Their outer clothing ('cowls and tunics') should be somewhat better than what they usually wear." A humble person will not draw attention to himself by what he wears, not even by its being shabby, ill-fitting, or in poor repair.

Chapter 55 concludes with the model all Christians should try to follow: "Yet the abbot should always keep in mind the sentence from the Acts of the Apostles that 'distribution was made to each according as anyone had need.' " Then he adds a typically humane consideration: "In this manner, therefore, let the abbot consider the weaknesses of the needy and not the ill-will of the envious. But in all his decisions let him think about the retribution of God." For reasons which may be either physical or psychological, some individuals need more than others in the way of material things. Let the abbot adapt his decisions to the makeup of each; those who have less because they need less should not grumble about it; those who need more, should be humbled by it. A humble person admits his own limitations and imperfections. Elsewhere Benedict writes: "He who needs less should thank God and not be discontented; but he who needs more should be humbled by the thought of his infirmity rather than feeling important on account of the kindness shown him. Thus all the members will be at peace" (*Rule* 34). Everyone in a community, from the abbot down, should be very concerned to be at peace.

As for literally "considering oneself a bad and worthless workman," to consider one's work worthless might not be so far from the truth as considering it indispensable, at the opposite pole. But many a reader might consider one extreme as bad as the other. "I am well trained, I am conscientious, I do a good job," you might say, of your work as a doctor, nurse, lawyer, policeman, janitor, construction worker, or whatever you do, and hopefully you are perfectly right. And you are committing no sin of pride in feeling that way, provided you acknowledge your dependence on God. Humility and common sense easily recognize that without the Creator who gives us our natural powers and our very existence, and without countless teachers, and others who supply the equipment and materials we use, our work would truly be bad. In fact we could get nothing done at all.

If you have been able to follow Benedict this far but feel that the sixth degree is "far out" or "going too far" and begin to lose confidence in him, don't throw the book in the wastebasket but have a little patience. Let us imagine Benedict understands your problem and explains himself as follows.

He is not encouraging a competitive spirit, not even in the sense jokingly caricatured by a certain Benedictine as "competing for the humility prize." Surely he too encouraged his disciples to strive for excellence in what they did, and to develop the gifts they received from God—not out of pride but for the sake of the Giver and out of gratitude. In the parable of the talents, our Lord praised the two who used their talents to double them and condemned the one who buried his (cf. Mt 25:14-30). But the one who was given two did not complain about another being given five.

One has to admire families who raise their children (or abbots who guide their subjects) to excel in whatever field their talents lie, like the family which has three members on the same major league baseball team: the father is a coach, his two sons play on the team, and one has already been named Most Valuable Player in the league. But when professional athletes begin vying with one another over salaries, then Benedict might fear "lest the sin of avarice creep in" (*Rule* 57), or vanity, over money as a status symbol. But he would subscribe to the Old Testament proverb, warning that "pride goes before a fall." There once was a lawyer who wanted to be "the best in New York." What he thought of as "the best" was "the richest." He was so successful that he rose to be United States Attorney General; but some of his practice as Attorney General led him onto the wrong side of the Court and from there to prison.

Benedict does not encourage competitiveness, neither trying to outdo one's neighbor in excellence, nor in its opposite (as a "bad and worthless workman"). But he does not discourage trying to do our work as well as we can. Nowadays there is less reason for making comparisons between the works themselves; the comparisons get made more in terms of salary; Benedict would challenge us to be content with less than others if we have enough and not look down on those who have less. In our push-button society, it is not so easy or realistic to compare the work we do using modern technology with the same kind of work done by others, with the same technology. But a humble man will not insist on having the very best equipment, if economic considerations make it necessary to make do with less. In the ancient world, where work was done by hand with simple tools, every job was very much your own, something like the comparison between the work of artists. Production is depersonalized but more efficient economically, when it is mass-produced or uses technology. Handwritten manuscripts could be more beautiful and took more skill than those we produce with word-processors and photocopiers. Laying stones (hand-carved sometimes) and bricks, in construction work, depended almost exclusively on individuals' skills, more than pouring cement or assembling a prefabricated home, barn, or warehouse today. Saint Gregory's *Life and Miracles of Saint Benedict* tells of a wall falling in and crushing one of the monastic laborers in the construction of Monte Cassino. His remains were carried in a sack to Benedict, who restored the monk to life. The mishap would have had to be blamed on the stonemasons' carelessness or lack of technical proficiency, but when accidents happen today, machinery is more often to blame than the incompetence of "bad and worthless" workmen.

Cooking over an open fire took more skill than using a microwave; housecleaning with a vacuum cleaner is easier than with primitive brooms, and today there is not so great a difference between the work an experienced janitor does and the work of a novice, nor can any individual be given much credit or blame for the way one vacuum cleaner performs compared with another; among the broom-makers at Monte Cassino there were no doubt some who had more cause than others for humility or vanity about their products. Two paperhangers today would not have so much reason to rival each other as two mural painters.

Since what he thinks of as the monk's principal work is work of a more spiritual nature, that is, primarily prayer, Benedict would probably apply this degree of humility more to that kind of work. We can hardly think of comparing this sort of work to that of others (who but God knows how well another person prays?); we compare it more with the ideal of how it should be done in order to be worthy of its object, God himself. It is when I am engaged in liturgical prayer (the kind of prayer to which the Rule devotes the most time) that I can easily feel "without understanding, become as a beast of burden," that is, comparable to the donkey on which Jesus entered Jerusalem on Palm Sunday. I may be truly carrying the Word of God by singing or reading it and hence doing marvelous work, but my lack of understanding or appropriate feeling makes me feel "bad and worthless as a workman, and brought to nothing." For this reason, the Church has us make our prayer end with the words, "through Christ our Lord." As a monk has no money but may be permitted to send a certain amount to, say, some charity or for the purchase of new books, the check has no value unless it carries the signature of the abbot; so our poor prayers acquire divine value in the ears of the Father when signed, as it were, with the name of his Son.

This degree of humility is less a virtue the monk strives to acquire by his own efforts, than a disposition, or frame of mind, brought about by the workings of grace in the soul. Where our effort and cooperation comes in, is more in not being discouraged by it. It is something like the "Night of the Senses" described by John of the Cross, a great sixteenth century teacher of the spiritual life. It is also not unlike the feelings of a great artist, the composer Verdi, for example, or of a great theologian, like Thomas Aquinas, who felt at the end of their lives that they had written nothing of real value. Verdi's conception of Beauty and Aquinas' of God were so sublime, that what they had written to express it seemed woefully inferior.

People entering seriously into the spiritual life, entering a monastery for example, love it at first; they feel good about what they are doing: they find the life of prayer a whole new experience and a very good one; they lap up spiritual books like a kitten at a saucer of milk; they like living with other religious people. And then everything seems to go wrong. Like a person moving to a new country, who reaches a plateau in learning its language after making fast progress for the first few months, then finds he or she does not seem able to learn any more; people new to the spiritual life reach a point where they do not feel they are getting better but think that they are even retrogressing. In part it is because the novelty has worn off. They are distressed by stronger temptations than they had ever felt; against faith and charity, for instance; or against patience with tiresome people, and against courage, as they see how far they have to go, and what a steep and daunting climb it is going to be. Prayer becomes more difficult and brings the soul little or no satisfaction. But actually they are by no means getting worse, though that is the way it feels; they are getting to know themselves and God better. God is revealing the shallowness of their previous faith, revealing their lack of charity, which was never before put to the test of living close to people very different from themselves, long enough for others' faults, limitations, and not-so-admirable idiosyncracies to begin to appear. (Jungian psychology says that what we dislike most in other persons is the "shadow" of our own personality.) It is not that they are going out of the light into darkness, but more like the eyes beginning to adjust to stronger light and seeing some of the weaknesses in themselves or ugliness formerly unsuspected. God does not lead us toward union with him in order to reveal our own holiness rather than his.

The soul's journey may be compared to a journey on foot through a forest, approached through a beautiful park; when we enter the forest, all kinds of fierce creatures emerge that we never knew were there. But they were hidden in our soul, not to mention the soul's enemies prowling in the forest. "Stay sober and alert," warns the apostle Peter. "Your opponent the devil is prowling like a roaring lion looking for someone to devour. Resist him, solid in your faith, realizing that the brotherhood of believers is undergoing the same sufferings throughout the world" (1 Pt 5:8-9). "But do not be at once dismayed and fly away from the way of salvation," we have already heard Benedict say (in the Prologue). You feel "brought to nothing," but you must stay faithful to God and remain solid in faith that he is with you. "I am brought to nothing," but "I am always with you." "Here I is! I ain't much, but I'se all I is," says Adam falling on his knees, whenever he hears the Lord calling, in the book *Ole Man Adam and His Chillun*, compiled many years ago on the basis of listening to the preaching of Baptist ministers to simple congregations in the South. In other words, "I am always with you, though I am brought to nothing."

Perhaps "the ground" was a symbol of the soul, and the "thorns and thistles" stood for the difficulties and contradictions the soul would meet in itself, when the author of Genesis (3:17-19) wrote, "Cursed be the ground because of you [Adam]! In toil shall you eat its yield all the days of your life [feeling a bad and worthless workman]; thorns and thistles shall it bring forth to you, as you eat of the plants of the field. . . . Until you return to the ground, from which you were taken; for you are dirt, and to dirt you shall return."

Another aspect of the humble "being content with the poorest and worst of everything" in the work of the spiritual life, is that they do not demand or expect extraordinary graces, more than enough to achieve the degree of holiness the Father has chosen for them. Not everyone is called to achieve holiness conspicuous in the history of the Church, just as not every stone in a church's construction goes into the spire. "We don't have visions at Downside," is said to have been the simple retort of an English abbot, when a fervent novice reported an unusual personal experience.

> The seventh degree of humility is that he consider himself lower and of less account than anyone else, and this not only in verbal protestation but also with the most heartfelt inner conviction, humbling himself and saying with the prophet, "But I am a worm and no man, the scorn of men and the outcast of the people. After being exalted, I have been humbled and covered with confusion." And again, "It is good for me that you have humbled me, that I may learn your commandments." (*Rule* 7)

So he does not expect visions, the gift of working miracles, or accolades from his brethren and pats on the back from his abbot for having such gifts. "Not to wish to be called holy before one is holy; but first to be holy, that one may be truly so called," is another of the Instruments of Good Works. If he does not become a superior or achieve any distinction, he knows that "it is good for me that God has humbled me," otherwise I might not have "learned his commandments." In fact, if he is convinced that he is "lower and of less account than anyone else," he is deeply grateful to be included as it were on their team, or to be like a humble penny among the silver dollars in his abbot's pocket. This degree of humility is beautifully illustrated by the story of Sylvanus the Actor, which we will quote in the next chapter.

Sometimes it takes the form of feeling not only that "I am the scorn of men and the outcast of the people," but even that I have been cast out by God. Thus Jesus said he felt on the cross, and the ascent to union with him must also climb through this, "never despairing of God's mercy" (*Rule* 4, #72), never ceasing to believe in God's love.

What Benedict describes as the seventh step on the ladder of humility could easily be confused with "low self-esteem," which is not so much a false humility as a sick sort of humility: not what Benedict, or Christ, had in mind. Our Lord was certainly not unaware of who he was, or lacking in respect for himself; yet he could say, "Learn from me, for I am gentle and humble of heart" (Mt 11:29). It is his sort of humility we desire to be made our own.

Except for telling us "to honor [or respect] everyone [or all people]" (a quotation of 1 Pt 2:17, among the Instruments of Good Works), Benedict nowhere warns us against confusing this degree of humility with low self-esteem. (If we are to respect all human beings, presumably we do not exclude ourselves, unless we take literally the psalmist's phrase, "I am a worm and no man.") If Benedict was unaware of this problem, that would be understandable. It is a common problem in the modern world (which is much more aware of clinical psychology, anyway—practically its discoverer) but must have been rare in his. As a form of depression, its cause can be chemical, treatable with medicine; and that can occur in any culture. But its cause is more often the result of negative experience, especially that of being an unwanted child, or the child of divorced parents. Both were very rare in the ancient world. Not to want a child was unthinkable; people wanted nothing so much, not just for the child's own sake, but because they depended on their children to take care of them in their old age. They were a kind of insurance, a kind of social security. Who else would take care of a widow? Society needed them: in ancient Greece, a woman needed to bear six children before she was thirty, just to keep the nation's population up to its needed strength. Women looked upon childlessness as the greatest calamity that could befall them, in Israel practically as a disgrace. Even a slave was wanted and needed, and knew it.

Humility is the opposite of pride. But just as there is a sick sort of humility, there is a healthy sort of pride: self-esteem, knowing one is the work of the Master Artist. Benedict seems to take it for granted in his monks. They want the best for themselves, if they want "eternal life," and they believe they have been called to it by Almighty God. It is owed to them, because Christ has paid the price, not for himself—it was his by nature—but to acquire it for the rest of humanity.

God is love; he creates out of love, which means he wants his created beings to exist because he sees they are good (cf. Gn 1). If you believe that, you take pride in being one of his creations; you are not his only good creation but one among a countless multitude of unique created beings. They are all as good as you; or perhaps better, in the sense that you cannot be what they are. But they cannot be what *you* are either, or rather: what you are *meant* to be—because with the rest of the children of Adam and Eve, you have fallen from the original design. Confession (the fifth degree of humility) assumes an awareness of the ways one has fallen short of God's design, in thought, word, and deed. I can only be my true self, that is, what he means me to become, if I live up to that design; in other words, if I do his will and eventually arrive at the joy of union with him. Keeping his commandments means working to achieve this design. ("It is good for me that you have humbled me, that I may learn your commandments," that is, become what you meant me to be.) The patient sick with "low self-esteem" can hardly say "it is good for me."

There is another kind of false humility, from which the Rule of Benedict here wishes to protect us. It is a temptation for people who believe themselves (not without some evidence) to be very religious. They worship God and, in his presence, admit themselves to be nothing by comparison with him. But they imagine themselves to be far better than ordinary people and imagine God thinks of them the same way, like the Pharisee in the Temple (cf. p. 64). They are worshipping an imaginary God; their understanding of God is far from what Jesus has revealed. Nobody who knows the true God, immeasurably superior to us, can look down on his fellows, because he knows we are all nothings by comparison with him, and no nothing is greater than another. We do know that each nothing is infinitely lovable to God (a mystery and a paradox, but true) and therefore worthy of our respect. If you begin to feel yourself better than someone else, take it as a danger signal; you may be falling into the devil's subtle trap.

The devil is content to let us become more self-controlled and more prayerful, if he can use this cure of relatively minor illnesses to infect us with a transfusion of the fatal virus of pride. He lets us invest a hundred dollars worth of imaginary humility, to gain a thousand dollars worth of pride toward our fellow humans, looking down on them as not so gifted, poorer because they seem irreligious or less religious, as less intelligent and therefore, in our eyes, as bores. This is the "humility" of a religious snob. It is easy for monastics or clergy to fall into it.

But for some people, as we have explained above, it would be wiser and healthier not to think of themselves as "lower and of lesser account than anyone else . . . 'a worm and no man.' "Benedict would try to heal them, by finding ways to affirm the goodness of their existence. It would be better for them not to be in a monastery, if nobody there could heal their broken spirit.

> The eighth degree of humility is that a monk do nothing except what is commended by the common Rule of the monastery and the example of the elders. (*Rule* 7)

This step is understandable enough, in the light of what has preceded it. To try to outdo others in the number of works undertaken, the amount of time spent in prayer, or by extraordinary penances is to attempt to be better than they, to be able to look down on them. We have already seen that this spirit of competitiveness is contrary to humility. It can be motivated too by a kind of exhibitionism, when done in order to be seen: "When you are praying, do not behave like the hypocrites who love to stand and pray in synagogues or on street corners in order to be noticed. . . . Whenever you pray, go to your room, close your door, and pray to your Father in private. . . . When you fast, you are not to look glum as the hypocrites do. They change the appearance of their faces so that others may see they are fasting. . . . When you fast, see to it that you groom your hair and wash your face. In that way no one can see you are fasting but your Father who is hidden and your Father who sees what is hidden will repay you" (Mt 6:5, 6, 16-18).

You are supposed to be praying all the time anyway, in the sense that you are consciously living in God's presence and for him. If you are living in order to impress your fellows, you spoil everything, as you are no longer living for God alone. If you get this right, as likely as not, others will be aware of it, and your life will be a better influence than most sermons, but you will be the last person to know it. This is made more explicit in the twelfth degree of humility.

Any number of saints have told us it does not matter what you do, what is important is the spirit in which it is done. So just do what everybody else does, in a humble spirit—with this proviso: that you imitate "what is *commended* by the common Rule and the example of the elders." There may be elements of the example given, by at least some of the elders, which are not commended and therefore are not to be imitated. One excuse for bad behavior is as old as the human race: "everybody does it," or at least "so-and-so does it." Adam tried to put the blame on Eve, "whom you yourself gave me as a partner," he has the insolence to say to the Lord God. Eve blames the serpent: "He tricked me," as if to say, "It's not my fault; it was not my own idea" (cf. Gn 3:12-13). Come on! We know that nothing excuses disobeying the commandment of God, not even the example or the commandment of a religious superior, or of one's spouse—let alone of the serpent.

> The ninth degree of humility is that a monk restrain his tongue
> and keep silence, not speaking until he is questioned. For the
> scripture shows that "in much speaking there is no escape from sin"
> and that "the talkative man is not stable on the earth." (*Rule* 7)

The Instruments of Good Works include: "To guard one's tongue against evil and depraved speech. Not to love much talking."

In our chapter on the Prologue, we have already seen Benedict's mind on this subject, and that even Shakespeare agreed with him. In the same place, we saw what he repeats in the next step: "The tenth degree of humility is that he be not ready and quick to laugh, for it is written, 'The fool lifts up his voice in laughter.' " Humility does not include playing the fool. Monastic life is centered around very serious things: prayer and reading the Word of God. It is in bad taste, irreverent, to look for ways in which they lend themselves to jokes. It is demeaning, and therefore incompatible with reverence and humility in their regard, to make fun of one's brethren, especially of the abbot. Notice that Benedict does not rule out all laughter here but precisely "being ready and quick to laugh," that is, being on the lookout for things and people to make fun of. It is not easy to poke fun without virtue going out from someone, as Monsignor Ronald Knox pointed out somewhere (himself endowed with a tremendous sense of humor: more often than not, directed at himself, which surely can be compatible with humility). Humble people do not take themselves too seriously. And some people have a delightful gift for the kind of humor that refreshes their neighbors and contributes to a fraternal spirit of cheerfulness, without being unkind or disrespectful. Benedict could approve of that, for it is not useless. The Rule encourages us in fact, "not to speak *useless* words or words that move to laughter" (*Rule* 4, #54). But pagan Rome was somewhat given to coarse humor, which Benedict banned at all times and places, as we saw in our chapter on the Prologue. The Rule further states: "Not to love much or boisterous laughter" (*Rule* 4, #55).

> The eleventh degree of humility is that when a monk speaks he do so gently and without laughter, humbly and seriously, in few and sensible words, and that he be not noisy in his speech. It is written, "A wise man is known by the fewness of his words." (*Rule* 7)

This continues the theme of the last two degrees: speaking with the reverence due to the presence of God, of which the humble are always aware.

> The twelfth degree of humility is that a monk not only have humility in his heart but also by his very appearance make it always manifest to those who see him. That is to say that whether he is at the Work of God, in the oratory, in the monastery, in the garden, on the road, in the fields or anywhere else, and whether sitting, walking or standing, he should always have his head bowed and his eyes toward the ground. Feeling the guilt of his sins at every moment, he should consider himself already present at the dread Judgment and constantly say in his heart what the publican in the gospel said with his eyes fixed on the earth: "Lord, I am a sinner and not worthy to lift up my eyes to heaven."[1] And again with the prophet: "I am bowed down and humbled everywhere."
>
> Having climbed all these steps of humility, therefore, the monk will presently come to that perfect love of God which casts out fear. And all those precepts which formerly he had not observed without fear, he will now begin to keep by reason of that love, without any effort, as though naturally and by habit. No longer will his motive be the fear of hell but rather the love of Christ, good habit and delight in the virtues which the Lord will deign to show forth by the Holy Spirit in his servant now cleansed from vice and sin. (*Rule* 7)

This is the top of the ladder, the ultimate goal which makes the upward struggle worthwhile: to be "cleansed from sin," arriving at "perfect love of God and of Christ, good habit and delight in the virtues," which is far superior

---

1. This is essentially the "Jesus Prayer," which Eastern Christians say with a kind of rosary—very "Benedictine," one could say.

to what human nature itself can achieve, but "the Holy Spirit will show it forth."

The test of perfect humility is not just seeing ourselves as unable to look down on anyone but living in the presence of God and Christ, so in love with them that you forget about yourself. Actually, this means humility gets left behind; you will no longer need the ladder when you have reached what the gospel means by love.

Until we get there, beware of the spiritual cancer of pride: it eats up common sense as well as love and contentment. But do not get discouraged; be confident that you will make it if you persevere. There is a lovely story, a true one, of an older monk in a French monastery in the 1920's, observing to a young novice, perhaps inclined to judge his brethren: "There are novices who seem to be saints, but they are not. There are middle-aged monks who do not seem to be saints, and they aren't. There are elderly monks who don't seem to be saints, but they are." The system works.

Sylvanus the Actor

In the last chapter of the Rule, Benedict says,

> We have written this Rule in order that by its observance in monasteries we may show that we have attained some degree of virtue and the rudiments of the religious life. But for him who would hasten to the perfection of that life there are the teachings of the holy Fathers, the observance of which leads a man to the height of perfection. For what page or what utterance of the divinely inspired books of the Old and New Testaments is not a most unerring rule for human life? Or what book of the holy Catholic Fathers does not loudly proclaim how we may come by a straight course to our Creator? Then the *Conferences* and the *Institutes* and the *Lives* of the Fathers, as also the Rule of our holy Father Basil—what else are they but tools of virtue for right-living and obedient monks?

The *Conferences* and the *Institutes* are the writings of John Cassian, recording the teaching and customs of the monks of Egypt at the end of the fourth century, from which Benedict drew a great deal. The *Lives* of the Fathers also tell mostly about the example of the early monks of Egypt. From a collection called *The Paradise of the Holy Fathers* we draw the story of Sylvanus the Actor, as an example of the monastic humility Benedict had in mind.

> Once there was a man among the brethren whose name was Sylvanus,who for a period of twenty years had worn the garb of a monk; now he was originally an actor, and at the beginning of his life as a monk he was exceedingly anxious about his soul, but after a short time had lapsed he began to be so negligent about his redemption, that he wanted to make merry and to enjoy himself, and besides this he used to sing fearlessly among the brethren snatches of the lewd and ribald songs which he used to hear in the theater. Then Abba Pachomius, the holy man, called this brother before the brethren and commanded him to strip off the garb of a monk and,

having received such apparel as was worn in the world, to go forth
from among the brethren and from the monastery. And that brother
fell down at the feet of Pachomius and entreated him, saying, "O
father,if you will forgive me this once, and will not cast me forth,
you have it from me that from this time forward I will repent of
those things wherein I have hitherto shown negligence, in such a
manner that you shall be able to see the change which has taken
place in my soul."

And the holy man answered and said to him, "Do you know how
much I have borne from you, and how many times I have admon-
ished you, and how many times I have beaten you? I am a man who
has no wish to stretch out my hands in a matter of this kind, because
when, of necessity, I was obliged to act thus in respect of you, my
soul suffered far more by the mention of association with passion
than you did, although the stripes were laid upon you. I beat you for
the sake of your salvation in God, so that by that means I might be
able to correct you of your folly; but since even though I admon-
ished you, you did not change your course of life, and did not follow
after spiritual excellence even though I entreated you so to do, and
since even when beaten you were not afraid, how is it possible for
me to forgive you any more?"

But when Sylvanus multiplied his entreaties, and begged for his
forgiveness long and earnestly, and promised that he would amend
his life, Rabba demanded a surety from him that after he was
forgiven he would no more continue his evil behavior; and when
the venerable man Petronius had made himself a surety for him
concerning the things which Sylvanus had promised, the blessed
man forgave him. Then Sylvanus, having been held worthy of
forgiveness, contended with all his soul, and to such good purpose,
that he became the pattern of all excellence of the fear of God, both
among all the younger and all the elder brethren. Now the virtue
which surpassed all the other virtues which he possessed was that
of absolute humility, and tears flowed from his eyes so unceasingly
that even when he was eating with the brethren he was not able to
restrain his weeping, and his tears were mingled with his food. And
when the brethren told him that he should not behave thus before
the face of strangers [i.e., visitors], or before any people, he took an

oath, saying, "I have sought many times to restrain my tears for this reason, but I have never been able to do so. " Then the brethren said, "Is it not possible for him that repents to seek to be alone? And would it not be better for him to act thus when he was praying with the brethren than when he was eating at the table with them? And is it not possible for the soul to weep continually with tears other than those which are visible?" Then turning to him, they said, "We wish to know what you have to say on the matter. For you are so overwhelmed with your tears that many of us who see you in this state are ashamed to eat and take our fill. "

Then Sylvanus said to those who had asked him those questions, "Do you not wish me to weep when I see holy men waiting upon me, men, the dust of whose feet I am unworthy to sweep away? Is it not proper that I should weep over myself? I weep then, O my brethren, because a man from the theater is ministered unto by such holy men as these, and I am afraid lest I be smitten even as were Dathan and Abiram [who rebelled against Moses and Aaron, cf. Num 16]. And I weep especially because, being in ignorance, I cared so little at the beginning about the salvation of my soul, that I came in danger of being expelled by the brethren from the monastery, and I was obliged to give surety for my better behavior, and to take awful oaths that I would never again treat my life with contempt. For this reason I am not ashamed to weep, and I have turned away from such things; for I know my sins and that if I was obliged to deliver up my soul I should find no happiness in heaven. "

And as this man strove nobly in this manner Rabba himself bore testimony before God that, "from the time when this monastery came into existence, among all the brethren who have lived with me therein, there has been none who has resembled completely the example which I have conceived in my mind with the exception of one. " Now when the brethren heard these things some of them thought that the one man of whom he spoke was Theodore, and others thought he was Petronius, and others thought he was Arsenius, and at length Theodore asked the holy man of which monk he had spoken when he said this thing; but Rabba did not wish to say. But because Theodore and the other great fathers continued to entreat him to tell them, for they wished to learn who he was, Rabba answered and said, "If I knew that vainglory would come to him of whom I am about to speak, and that he would be greatly praised, I would not show you who he is; but, because I know that the more he is praised, the more humble he will become, and the more he will think scorn of himself, and because I wish you to emulate his example, I will, before you all, fearlessly ascribe blessing to him. You, O Theodore, and all those, who like you, strive in the fight, have bound the Calumniator with fetters like a kid of the goats, and have placed him under your feet, and daily you trample upon him as you trample upon dust; but if you are the least unmindful of yourselves, the Calumniator, who has been cast under your feet, will rise up again and will set himself against you like an armed man. But this young man Sylvanus, who but a short time since was about to be expelled from the monastery, has, by his strenuousness, so completely subjugated the Calumniator and slain him, that he will never again be able to approach him, for he has vanquished him utterly by his exceedingly great humility. You have humbled your-selves as if you possessed works of righteousness, and the addition which you would make to your spiritual excellence is reduced, for you rely upon the things which have already been performed by you; but this young man, however much he strives, never shows himself to the gaze of his fellows, and he thinks with all his mind and soul that he is a useless and contemptible being. And tears are always nigh unto him because he is always belittling himself, and because he says that he is unworthy of the things which are visible. You, in your knowledge, and in your patient endurance, and in your strivings against the Calumniator, which cannot be measured, are better than he is, but he has surpassed you in humility, because he, in this manner, cuts off for the Calumniator nothing but humility, and the power of action which arises from the whole soul." Now therefore when Sylvanus had striven in this manner for eight years, he completed his fight, and laid down his life in such wise that his servant, a mighty man of God, testified concerning his departure, and said that an endless throng of holy angels, with great rejoicing and singing, received his soul as a choice sacrifice, and that they offered it up unto God like the marvelous incense which is found among the children of men.

Benedict's teaching on humility is based on his understanding of the relation of the soul to God. Before going on to his teaching on prayer, by which the soul articulates this relationship, it is fitting to remind the reader of Mary's "Magnificat," in which the greatest and humblest of God's creatures gives incomparable expression to the sentiments of this virtue. It might be called "The Canticle of Humility" and is easier to understand having Benedict's scriptural doctrine on humility fresh in the mind:

My being proclaims the greatness of the Lord,
my spirit finds joy in God my savior,
For he has looked upon his servant in her humility;
all ages to come shall call me blessed.
God who is mighty has done great things for me,
holy is his name;
His mercy is from age to age
on those who fear him.
He has shown might with his arm;
he has confused the proud in their inmost thoughts.
He has deposed the mighty from their thrones
and raised the lowly to high places.
The hungry he has given every good thing,
while the rich he has sent empty away.
He has upheld Israel his servant,
ever mindful of his mercy;
Even as he promised our fathers,
promised Abraham and his descendants forever.

As scriptural reading we also recommend the First Letter of Peter; from frequent quotes it is clearly a source for Benedict's teaching on humility and obedience.

Prayer

Private Prayer

Benedict had a special genius for designing a blueprint for Christian community life; his is a "community" spirituality. What we have seen so far has been directed at individuals, but with a view to guiding them into relating well not only to God but also to each other, in God. Most of what Benedict writes about prayer is concerned with community prayer, but we will start with his brief but very pregnant words about the individual's communication of his heart to God—without which community prayer would be superficial and risk being mere show:

> First of all, whatever good work you begin to do, beg of him [the Lord Christ] *with most earnest prayer* to perfect it, that he who has now deigned to count us among his sons may not at any time be grieved by our evil deeds. (*Rule,* Prol.)

It is hard to keep an element of evil from entering our deeds, unless they are preceded by prayer and carried out in a prayerful spirit, that is, with reverence for God and under the inspiration of grace. Benedict is suggesting that everything we do should start with the petition of the Lord's Prayer, "Thy will be done" and with a humble acknowledgement that it will not be done to God's satisfaction without his help.

> When we wish to suggest our wants to men of high station, we do not presume to do so except with humility and reverence. How much the more, then, are complete humility and pure devotion necessary in supplication of the Lord who is God of the universe! And let us be assured that it is not in saying a great deal that we shall be heard but in purity of heart and in tears of compunction. Our prayer, therefore, ought to be short and pure, unless it happens to be prolonged by an inspiration of divine grace. (*Rule* 20)

Chapter 52, "On the Oratory of the Monastery" applies also to community prayer ("the Work of God") but is concerned mostly about private prayer and the importance of having a place where the individual can pray in peace, when so inclined.

Let the oratory be what it is called, a place of prayer; and let nothing else be done there or kept there. When the Work of God is ended, let all go out in perfect silence, and let reverence for God be observed, so that any brother who may wish to pray privately will not be hindered by another's misconduct. And at other times also, if anyone should want to pray by himself, let him go in simply and pray, not in a loud voice but with tears and fervor of heart. He who does not say his prayers in this way, therefore, shall not be permitted to remain in the oratory when the Work of God is ended, lest another be hindered. (*Rule* 50)

The simple instruction on prayer in chapter 20 starts with another of Benedict's exhortations to reverence before God and to humility, adding the hope that prayer will be made with "pure devotion and purity of heart." God is referred to as "the Lord God of all things": not just the God of Abraham, Isaac, and Jacob; nor the God of Christians alone, but "the God of all," a phrase expressing awareness of the universality of God's creative power, providence, and love. Prayer is to be made "with humility and reverence," analogous to the humility and reverence with which Benedict recognizes we approach persons "of high station" or the rich (who win respect by the very fear they inspire, as he says in chapter 53, "On the Reception of Guests").

But why does such a sober, realistic writer as Benedict, limiting his words to a few essential guidelines for praying well, recommend praying "with tears," in order to get heard? "Tears of compunction": compunction is defined as remorse, regret for some wrong, and "poignant uneasiness proceeding from a sense of guilt." "Tears" sound like sentimentality, which is totally absent from the rest of the Rule. Sentimentality is emotion in excess of what its object merits, cultivated perhaps for its own sake, out of a kind of spiritual sensuality. This is not what he is recommending. Tears are a natural, appropriate response to an encounter with real holiness.

Sometimes this awareness of the holy comes through a spiritual song; through sacred music with or without words; or in meeting a really holy person: we realize we are encountering the supernatural, infinitely distant from our pathetic degree of faith and virtue, infinitely more "real," as it were. Some authors convey it in their books. C. S. Lewis, for example, does so in

The Chronicles of Narnia by his description of "Aslan" (the lion who is obviously an image of Christ, of whom the author must have had a deep experience). Many are moved in this way by Francis' description of "Perfect Joy" in the *Fioretti*, or by such poignant biblical stories as the lament of David for his son Absalom (2 Sm 19:1) or the story of the "Good Thief," in Luke's account of the crucifixion. Benedict would have us call to mind, when we pray, anything which moves us this way, because it brings us closer to an awareness of God as he really is, and consequently we pray better.

Those are ordinary graces, if any grace can be called "ordinary." Not many have such extraordinary graces as Bernadette's vision of Our Lady at Lourdes. "I could have stayed there forever, looking at *her*," Bernadette said later. "She is so lovely that, when you have seen her once, you would willingly die to see her again." At the second apparition, when Bernadette went into ecstasy, some adults present thought she was dead; being unable to carry her away, they sent for the miller's son, a strapping fellow of twenty-eight. "*Tears were streaming from her eyes,*" he told later. " She was smiling and her face was lovelier than anything I've ever seen." Bernadette found joy enough to move her to tears and make her totally unaware of the world around her, because she saw Our Lady alive, smiling at her and inviting her to come nearer. The only joy greater than that would be to see God himself; but through his mother, Bernadette saw beauty sharing in and reflecting the divine, and when we see photographs or films taken of other visionaries at the moment of an apparition, we can get an inkling of what they saw.

It is quite normal to experience a similar response when we seriously contemplate the Person of the Crucified: the personification of the rejection of God's love. How can Life die? *For us!* Reflect on what his mother must have been feeling, in the light of her memories, of her knowledge of who he was, and of her expectation of life without him. There are pictures and poems which capture this, especially liturgical hymns and prayers, for instance the Lamentations sung on Good Friday night in the Byzantine liturgy: artistic representation of the passion of Christ moves us to sorrow and to joy: joy that Christ loves us so much, sorrow at the many ways he has been rejected. Even in the natural order, there are people whose strength of character, usually at the expense of tremendous suffering borne nobly over a long period of time, reaches the stature of the heroic; to meet them or to read of them, or of some tragic figure in fact or fiction (Shakespeare's King Lear, for example, or Romeo and Juliet), cannot help occasioning tears of admiration or compassion.

The Bible is not without examples of "prayer with tears." The Psalter, for instance, which is the prayer-book inspired by God himself and given to us to suit practically any occasion (cf. Ps 6:43 and 137). And then the Lamentations of Jeremiah, an inspired response to the sight of the humiliation of God's people: the Temple destroyed, its ritual interrupted, the Holy City depopulated, the weakness of sinful people who had merited this, contrasted with the fidelity of the God their sins had betrayed. We can apply this to other past or present situations in history, in the Church, the family, or one or another nation: "Bitterly she [the holy city] weeps at night. . . . Gone is all her glory. . . . At this I weep, my eyes run with tears. . . . Worn out with weeping are my eyes, because of the downfall of the daughter of my people, as child and infant faint away in the open spaces of the town. . . . Cry out to the Lord; moan, O daughter Zion! Let your tears flow like a torrent day and night. . . . Pour out your heart like water in the presence of the Lord. . . . For the Lord's rejection does not last forever; though he punishes, he takes pity, in the abundance of his mercies. . . . Let us reach out our hearts toward God in heaven . . . from the bottom of the pit! Lead us back to you, O Lord, that we may be restored" (Lam 1:2, 6, 16; 2:11, 18, 19; 3:31, 32, 41, 55; 5:21). It is powerful stuff; and it shows there is a rock-solid foundation in scripture for Benedict's advice to pray "in tears of compunction."

Many Benedictine congregations today, adapting to modern circumstances and the wisdom of later religious orders, schedule a set amount of time in the day for private prayer. Benedict does not. As we will see later, he schedules a good deal of time for *lectio divina* ("spiritual reading" or "reading which has to do with God"), but of time devoted to private prayer he simply says it should "be short and pure, unless it happens to be prolonged by an inspiration of divine grace." *Lectio divina* would be included today in what is called "meditation," but Benedict advises us to follow our heart, or the invitation of the Spirit dwelling in our hearts, in choosing for ourselves when to engage in the kind of prayer that uses no text but arises spontaneously, without trying to prolong it longer than it lasts of itself. He does not encourage sitting idly around waiting for some inspiration to come but would obviously encourage praying for it when one feels the need.

It is a very natural need for people to feel, and in the chapter "On the Oratory," Benedict shows he understands that one needs a place for it; he does not allot each monk a room of his own, where he can "close his door, and pray to his Father in private" (cf. Mt 6:6); he provides an Oratory and prescribes that it "be what it is called" (the term comes from the Latin *orare,* "to pray"). He says something similar of the abbot, "who . . . should always remember what he is called" (*Rule* 2), and chapter 4 applies the same let-it-be-what-it-is-called philosophy to the individual person: "Not to wish to be called holy before one is holy; but first to be holy, that one may be truly so called." It seems to have been a favorite expression of Benedict's, a favorite thought: that things should be what they are called. One of his sons, giving a retreat conference some fourteen centuries later, used a similar refrain, "Be what you are, and you are bound to grow." Let an oratory be what its name implies. It must be a silent place, with a silence based on reverence for the presence of God, conducive to prayer. "Let nothing else be done there or kept there." It is not the place for choir practices, lectures, or recreation. Just what one might be tempted to keep there, he does not specify; it is not to be used as a tool shed, animal shelter, or storeroom, that is for sure; he would not make this ban if he had not found monks being quite inventive in the uses they might find for it. He provided for problems he could hardly have imagined, arising from Abbey churches becoming tourist attractions: architectural sights, museums of fine art, or shrines drawing thousands of pilgrims because of the presence of miraculous statues and icons and saints' tombs—circumstances which required monasteries to construct or adapt other spaces for private prayer, visitors to the Abbey church not always making it a place conducive to prayer outside of public ceremonies.

It is a challenge to many city-dwellers today to find such a place of stillness, if one's home or apartment is not large enough to set aside one room, and nearby churches or chapels have to be kept locked for fear of vandals. Whether or not *The Education of Little Tree,* by Forrest Carter is an authentic autobiographical memoir of a Cherokee's childhood (some critics have questioned it), it is an authentic expression of people's need for some such "secret place," whatever their religion may be:

"Following the spring branch was how I found the secret place. It was a little ways up the side of the mountain and hemmed in with laurel. It was not very big, a grass knoll with an old sweet gum tree bending down. When I saw it, I knew it was my secret place, and so I went there a whole lot.

"I reckoned I was too young to keep a secret, for I had to tell Grandma about my place. She wasn't surprised—which surprised me. Grandma said all Cherokees had a secret place. . . . Grandma said it was necessary. Which made me feel right good about having one.

"Grandma said everybody has two minds. One of the minds has to do with the necessaries for body living. . . . But she said we had another mind that had nothing at all to do with such. She said it was the spirit mind. . . . Grandma said that the spirit mind was like any other muscle. If you used it it got bigger and stronger. She said the only way it could get that way was using it to understand, but you couldn't open the door to it until you quit being greedy and such with your body mind. . . .

"Natural, she said, understanding and love was the same thing; except folks went at it backwards too many times, trying to pretend they loved things when they didn't understand them. Which can't be done."[1]

Community Prayer

We come now to what Benedict writes about community prayer, which he calls "the Work of God" (*Opus Dei* in Latin), of which *Perfectae Caritatis* says: "The main task of monks is to render to the Divine Majesty a service at once simple and noble, within the monastic confines" (#9). To this subject Benedict devotes about twenty percent of the chapters in his Rule, which shows how much importance he attached to it. His community is a "house of God," God dwells there, especially in his Word. The Work of God consists in the reading (out loud of course), or chanting, of the Word of God, and of a few ecclesiastical compositions based on the Word, like hymns or commentaries. The importance of this is easily understood, once we realize that not everyone in his community could read; therefore they were dependent on *hearing* it. God in his Word holds the whole community together and guides them. When we read the Word of God to others, and listen to it ourselves, we are doing "the work of God" in their souls and ours. This is why we have prayer groups and scripture-reading groups—besides regular liturgical functions, for which we show our appreciation by faithful and attentive participation, reflecting on the immense gift Jesus makes to us every time we meet in his name: his presence.

---

1. Forrest Carter, *The Education of Little Tree* (Albuquerque: University of New Mexico Press, 1976), pp. 58-60.

We believe that the divine presence is everywhere and that "the eyes of the Lord are looking on the good and the evil in every place." But we should believe this especially without any doubt when we are assisting at the Work of God. To that end let us be mindful always of the prophet's words, "Serve the Lord in fear" and again "Sing praises wisely" and "In the sight of the angels I will sing praise to you." Let us therefore consider how we ought to conduct ourselves in the sight of the Godhead and of his angels, and let us take part in the psalmody in such a way that our mind may be in harmony with our voice. (*Rule* 19)

A practical consequence of understanding the importance of this work is getting to it quickly and punctually, and making it the first thing to be done on the day's schedule. This is considered more important than the rule of not talking at night. ("Monks ought to be zealous for silence at all times, but especially during the hours of the night," *Rule* 42). Therefore "when they rise for the Work of God let them gently encourage one another, that the drowsy may have no excuse" (*Rule* 22). They are to get into the oratory quickly when the signal is given, like passengers waiting in the departure lounge of an airport when their flight is announced. And throughout the day, "at the hour for the Divine Office, as soon as the signal is heard, let them abandon whatever they may have in hand and hasten with the greatest speed, yet with seriousness, so that there is no excuse for levity. Let nothing, therefore, be put before the Work of God" (*Rule* 43).

If anyone arrives late, he does not go to his usual place in the choir but to the last place, "or in a place set aside by the abbot for such negligent ones"—like the penalty box, beside an ice hockey rink.

The reason why we have judged it fitting for them to stand in the last place or in a place apart is that, being seen by all, they may amend for very shame. For if they remain outside the oratory, there will perhaps be someone who will go back to bed and sleep or at least seat himself outside and indulge in idle talk, and thus an occasion will be provided for the evil one. But let them go inside, that they may not lose the whole Office and may amend for the future. (*Rule* 43)

The whole day is interspersed with "Offices," that is, periods of prayer, to reinforce one's closeness to the Lord and remembrance of his Word.

"Seven times in the day," says the prophet, "I have rendered praise to you." Now that sacred number of seven will be fulfilled by us if we perform the Offices of our service at the time of the Morning Office, and at the first, third, sixth, and ninth hours, of Vespers and of Compline [which ended the day]. (*Rule* 16)

What is sacred about the number seven? Well, this subject would require a special article; many Fathers of the Church saw some spiritual significance in various numbers. This is the only time Benedict explicitly subscribes to it; but it is implicit elsewhere. For instance, there are seventy-two books in the Bible; it must be no coincidence that there are also seventy-two chapters to the Holy Rule, not counting the prologue and epilogue, and seventy-two Instruments of Good Works in chapter 4. There are mathematicians who tell us that there is more to this than just a quaint eccentricity.

The Romans did not use our clocks of twelve hours divided into sixty minutes each; with less precision they divided the day into twelve hours, and the night either into four watches or (as Benedict does) into twelve night hours. This means the hours were of different length in winter and summer. Today, Offices can be scheduled with precision, the signal given by an electrically timed bell; and if he has one, the monk can look at a clock or watch and see how much time he has. But in Benedict's day, the signal went when the abbot (or the person he assigned) chose to give it, and the monk had to stand ready to drop what he was doing. People who do not live in monasteries can imitate Benedict by taking time out for prayer at certain intervals. The "hours" of prayer interspersed through the work day were very brief. What Benedict calls the "Night Office" was said when the monks rose before daylight.

As for the Night Office, the same prophet says, "In the middle of the night I arose to glorify you." Let us therefore bring our tribute of praise to our Creator "for the judgments of his justice" at these times . . . and in the night let us arise to glorify him. (*Rule* 16)

Several chapters of the Rule are devoted to distributing all 150 psalms to the various Offices of the week.

We strongly recommend, however, that if this distribution of the psalms is displeasing to anyone, he should arrange them otherwise, in whatever way he considers better, but taking care in any case that the Psalter with its full number of 150 psalms be chanted every week. (*Rule* 18)[1]

The Psalter as the basic prayer-book was not an original idea with Benedict; he inherited it from the pioneering monks of Egypt. Quotations from them permeate the Rule, which can even be studied as a key to better understanding of the Psalter, or as a digest of its spirituality. "The time that remains [in the winter months] after the Night Office should be spent by those brethren who need a better knowledge of the Psalter or the lessons" (*Rule* 8). This "better knowledge" most probably consisted in memorizing the psalms and certain scripture passages which were said by heart in the Divine Office. Benedict does not mention this himself, but many Egyptian monks used to recite the psalms by heart at their labor of basket-weaving, which was not unlike that of a factory worker on an assembly line.

However greatly Benedict esteemed the psalms, the gospels were the books for which he had the most reverence. At the end of the Night Office on Sundays, "the abbot shall read the lesson from the book of the gospels, while all stand in reverence and awe" (*Rule* 11). When the gospels were read, it was as if the Lord himself were standing among them and speaking to them. All are also to "rise from their seats out of honor and reverence to the Holy Trinity, as soon as the 'Glory be to the Father' begins" (at the end of the "responsory" chanted after the last lesson of the Night Office) (*Rule* 9).

The books to be read at the Night Office shall be those of divine authorship, of both the Old and the New Testament, and also the explanations of them which have been made by well-known and orthodox Catholic Fathers. (*Rule* 9)

---

1. If you examine the Rule for the way Benedict distributed the psalms through the week, remember that the numbering he uses for the psalms is not the same as in most Bibles printed today. He uses the numbering of the official Latin and Greek versions (the Vulgate and the Septuagint); today most versions follow the numbering in our Hebrew text. In all, the total number is 150. Psalms 1-8 are identical and so are 148-150. What Benedict numbers as Psalm 9, in the Hebrew is divided, after 9:21, into Psalms 9 and 10. Consequently, Benedict's Psalm 10 is Psalm 11 in the Hebrew; Benedict's 11 is the Hebrew's 12, and so on. You add 1 to get the Hebrew numbering (e.g., 50-51) all the way to 145-146. Benedict's Psalm 146 corresponds to the Hebrew 147:1-11. Benedict's 147, to the Hebrew 147:12-20. From 148 the numbers coincide again.

Benedict wanted instruction, as a trustworthy guide to the kingdom of heaven, to be scriptural, catholic, and orthodox: three qualities which went naturally together in those days of the undivided Church.

The Morning Office was to include "a canticle from the prophets, each on its own day as chanted by the Roman Church," and "the canticle from the gospel book" (traditionally, the canticle of Zechariah, daily). The "canticle from the gospel book" prescribed for Vespers is traditionally that of Mary, the "Magnificat." Both are to be found in the first chapter of Luke (*Rule* 13, 17, 18).

> The Morning and Evening Offices should never be allowed to pass without the superior saying the Lord's Prayer in its place at the end so that all may hear it, on account of the thorns of scandal which are apt to spring up. Thus those who hear it, being warned by the covenant which they make in that prayer when they say, "Forgive us as we forgive," may cleanse themselves of faults against that covenant.[1] But at other Offices let the last part only of that prayer be said aloud, so that all may answer, "But deliver us from evil." (*Rule* 13).

Every Hour of prayer included the Lord's Prayer at its conclusion.

How seriously Benedict took the care with which the Work of God ought to be performed is reflected in chapter 45, "On Those Who Make Mistakes in the Oratory":

> When anyone has made a mistake while reciting a psalm, a responsory, an antiphon or a lesson, if he does not humble himself there before all by making a satisfaction,[2] let him undergo a greater punishment because he would not correct by humility what he did wrong through carelessness.[3] No one shall presume to sing or read unless he can fulfill that office in such a way as to edify the hearers. Let this function be performed with humility, gravity and reverence, and by him whom the abbot has appointed. (*Rule* 45 and 47)

This is not a bad principle to follow in choosing lectors for parish Masses; only those should be chosen who can read out loud in a way the congregation

---

1. Recall here what was said (on p. 59) commenting on the verse "he who has done no evil to his neighbor" in the Prologue.
2. Some sign of apology, like kneeling or bending down and touching the ground.
3. Each monk is expected to be his own referee, in calling "fouls."

can understand. Sing "with humility": Benedict does not want liturgical music to be used as an occasion for "prima donnas" to display their operatic voices, or musicians their virtuosity; liturgy is prayer, not a concert; yet it should "edify the hearers" by its beauty and its message, it should not be ugly or done carelessly. If done without "gravity and reverence," it would be unworthy of the honor due the Holy Trinity. Much depends on the motivation of the performers: if communal prayer is performed without pride, for *God's* glory, not the performers', then it cannot be performed too perfectly.

Benedict is a man of few words: he expressed the essentials of what is said on the subject in *Sacrosanctum Concilium*, the first Constitution of the Second Vatican Council, whose paragraphs 112-21 deal with Sacred Music ("sacred melody united to words") and its "ministerial function in the service of the Lord"; it ought to "accord with the dignity of the temple, and truly contribute to the edification of the faithful"; its purpose is "the glory of God and the sanctification of the faithful . . . by way of forming their attitude toward religion." "Sacred music increases in holiness to the degree that it winningly expresses prayerfulness and promotes solidarity."

The pastoral council was primarily concerned with liturgy's pastoral function; Benedict is primarily concerned with it as a need and a duty for persons who have chosen to live for God alone, a daily responsibility never to be neglected, and so he has rules for

> those brethren who are working at a great distance and cannot get to the oratory at the proper time—the abbot judging that such is the case. [They] shall perform the Work of God in the place where they are working, bending their knees in reverence before God. Likewise those who have been sent on a journey shall not let the appointed hours pass by, but shall say the Office by themselves as well as they can and not neglect to render the task of their service.

Benedict scheduled the hours for prayer, reading, work, eating, and sleeping in accord with the rhythms of nature (also in accord with the Church's liturgical year, which revolved around Easter and Pentecost as its culmination). This is extremely difficult to manage in the modern world, since our habits have been changed by the discovery of electricity, all but canceling the difference between day and night; but monks who have experimented with following his timetable exactly, have found that there are benefits to be gained from it.

In winter time, that is from the Calends of November [i.e., November 1] until Easter, the brethren shall rise at what is calculated to be the eighth hour of the night, so that they may sleep somewhat longer than half the night and rise with their rest completed. . . . From Easter to the aforesaid Calends of November, the hour of rising should be so arranged that the Morning Office, which is to be said at daybreak, will follow the Night Office after a very short interval. (*Rule* 8)

Benedict had his monks rise for prayer not much later than when today's TV-viewers go to bed, that is, about 2 A.M.

Even in Lent, i.e., before the vernal equinox, when the monks fast until the evening, the meal must be scheduled so that it will be taken before dark but after Vespers. Afterwards there is a period of public reading from Cassian's *Conferences*, followed by Compline. So they would go to sleep by about 7 P.M. and get seven hours of rest.

In Lent until Easter let them dine in the evening. But this evening hour shall be so determined that they will not need the light of a lamp while eating, but everything will be accomplished while it is still daylight. Indeed at all seasons let the hour for meals be so arranged that everything will be done by daylight. (*Rule* 41)

Does it make any difference, what time of the day or night we go to rest, or stay up to work, or whatever? The fact is, even in scripture, the hours of night are associated with evil: "Let us cast off deeds of darkness. . . . Let us live honorably as in daylight; not in carousing and drunkenness, not in sexual excess and lust, not in quarreling and jealousy. Rather, put on the Lord Jesus Christ" (Rom 13:12-14). "Light produces every kind of goodness and justice and truth. Take no part in vain deeds done in darkness; rather, condemn them. It is shameful even to mention the things these people do in secret. That is why we read: 'Awake, O sleeper, arise from the dead, and Christ will give you light' " (Eph 5:9, 11, 12, 14).

A lot of us in industrialized countries never see the sunrise. I do not mean the dawn as it comes to already lighted streets but as it breaks upon a rural, especially sylvan area. Deep, silent darkness gives way to increasing light and to the sounds of waking birds; often a gentle breeze stirs the trees out of their stillness. It is as though the whole earth were rising from the dead, gently. Many intellectuals who do not believe in Christ's resurrection in the

terms of the Nicene Creed, actually believe Easter was invented as a mythological way of celebrating the return of nature to life in the season of Spring,
unaware that the early Christians never thought of that but connected it with
Passover, the rising of the people of Israel out of foreign slavery into freedom
in their own land, a prophetic symbol of Christ leading humankind out of the
slavery of Satan and death into eternal life and the kingdom of heaven. One
suspects these intellectuals are the kind who burn the midnight oil over their
books and papers, or they could have witnessed the rebirth of daylight,
associated it with the story of Jesus rising from his tomb at the crack of dawn,
and imagined that the early Church invented the story of the first Easter as a
mythological celebration of light trampling down the night. Of all the effects
produced by the motion of the sun, the moon, and the earth in relation to each
other, the dawning of day is the most obvious symbol of the Resurrection of
the Light of the World. The "Ambrosian hymns," to be sung at Benedict's
Night and Morning Offices on Sunday, make this connection. (They were
attributed to Ambrose, fourth century bishop of Milan who converted
Augustine).

Phos hilaron ("O gladsome light"), the earliest known Christian hymn,
makes this connection too, but at sunset rather than sunrise, expressing faith
that Christ still lives as the glory of the immortal Father in heaven (after it
has set, the sun shines in another sky than our own). Like the setting sun,
Christ has disappeared from the earth, but the hymn implies the hope that he
will come again, that there will be a tomorrow.

Christians in some localities stay up all night to celebrate Easter every
Sunday morning. Benedict seems to have wanted his monks to see the coming
of day in this light. There is something holy about the early morning hour,
when Christ rose, and unholy about the darkness of night, the time when
thieves are abroad and other kinds of unhealthy or unethical behavior tend
to take place. So, very probably, Benedict deliberately occupied his people
with intervals of work and prayer from before daylight, with the pragmatic
purpose of getting them good and tired, and tucked away, by the time the
mischief of night begins.

If we wonder whether it is realistic of Benedict to assign about two and a
half hours a day to prayer (not counting the time assigned to holy reading),
remember that people commonly spend more time than that watching television. For one week, try spending as much time in his kind of prayer as,
otherwise, you might have spent on television: Pray the psalms (they become

so familiar that they seem like prayers of our own); add some reading of other parts of scripture and commentaries on it; end with the Our Father, after the Canticle of Zechariah in the morning, and the "Magnificat" in the evening; and ask yourself at the week's end if the time seems to have been wasted, compared with the value of TV or whatever else you may normally use to relax.

As regards the way to read or pray the scriptures, the way of the Catholic Church and of the Orthodox Churches of the East is not to read and interpret them in isolation from the rest of the Church, or from its ages-old tradition. This saves us from impatience with passages whose interpretation is, admittedly, somewhat mysterious even to scholars.

To suggest a family's life could be structured in some such way as this, is not out of tune either with Benedict or with the Church of today. Take for instance the words of Pope John Paul II on June 5, 1992 addressed to the faithful on his visit to Angola: "Look to the Holy Family of Nazareth! Look at the hidden life-style which the Son of God made man led, together with Mary and Joseph. The gospel says: 'He went down with them and came to Nazareth, and was obedient to them; and his mother kept all these things in her heart. And Jesus advanced in wisdom and age and favor before God and man' (Lk 2:51-52). May the Holy Family grant you this profound human and Christian maturity. *A necessary condition for this is that your home be a privileged place of prayer and living catechesis where your children are helped to grow in their supernatural vocation and trained in values worthy* of men and women. Then your family will truly be a 'domestic Church.' "

God

Prayer is the chief way of activating and developing one's humble relationship with God. But what does "God" mean to Benedict? To say he is the God of the Bible is too general a statement. In himself, the God of the Bible is beyond the comprehension of any human being, even of the greatest saints; all of them experienced him in their own ways, meeting him in their own contexts, relating less to some words than to others about him. Even in human relationships, every member of a person's family, and every friend, will see him or her in a different light. John is "my brother Jack" to one woman, "my parish priest" to another; and Robert may be "Uncle Bob" to one, "Father" to another, "Granddad" to another. "Beauty is in the eye of the beholder"; each beholder will respond to diverse aspects of the subject from a different angle, though each will recognize the other's perception as true and will be enriched by it.

The study of what God meant to a certain saint (or even to any person) can tell you much about him or her and can also appear as the foundation and explanation of the morals he or she exemplified and taught. The saints' concept of God contributes to the shape of their character, but their concept of God may itself be shaped somewhat by the times and the environment in which they lived. Teresa of Avila, for instance, regularly referred to God or to Christ as "His Majesty," a title that would have been meaningful and appropriate for a person who lived as she did, in sixteenth century Spain, under an absolute monarch; but to us who have grown up in a republic or under a constitutional monarchy, it is hard to relate to and may even be misleading or distasteful, unless we are familiar with her historical context. Reading the *Autobiography* of Thérèse of Lisieux, we can see that her faith and her spiritual life were wonderfully affected by the affection between her and her saintly father; we do not sense that the name "Father," applied to God, was charged with equal feeling for Augustine, when we read his *Confessions* or sermons.

In any case, let us collect Benedict's perceptions of God and of Christ (God incarnate); it will be worth a certain amount of repetition to review the texts in this light. To study any saint's notion of God can be beneficial to any

Christian, clarifying what we mean when we say "We believe in God," and purifying our faith of any false or defective ideas.

Ever Present

God is always present, not only "from afar" (heaven) but also "within our thoughts, minds, and hearts"; regardless of whether we are thinking of him or not, he is looking into us: "Let a man consider that God is always looking at him from heaven. . . . This is what the prophet shows us when he represents God as ever present within our thoughts, in the words 'Searcher of minds and hearts is God. . . .' As for the desires of the flesh, let us believe with the prophet that God is ever present to us, when he says to the Lord, 'Every desire of mine is before you' " (*Rule* 7). When the novice finally takes his vows, "this promise he shall make before God and his Saints, [i.e.] before all in the oratory" (*Rule* 58). (God is never alone; he is always accompanied by his saints and by the angels who report our actions to him.) One of the Instruments of Good Works is

> to know for certain that God sees one everywhere. Therefore since the eyes of the Lord observe the good and the evil, and the Lord is always looking down from heaven on the children of men "to see if there be anyone who understands and seeks God," and since our deeds are daily, day and night, reported to the Lord by the angels assigned to us, we must constantly beware, brethren, as the prophet says in the psalm, lest at any time God see us falling into evil ways and becoming unprofitable. (*Rule* 4 and 7)

Benedict believes there is a special presence of God in a monastery, particularly in the oratory and at the Work of God, for it is "his house."

> The proper times should be observed in giving the things that have to be given and asking for the things that have to be asked for, that no one may be troubled or vexed *in the house of God*. . . . Let the house of God be managed by prudent men and in a prudent manner. . . . If the community should agree to choose a person [to be abbot] who will acquiesce in their vices, and if those vices somehow become known to the bishop to whose diocese the place belongs, or to the abbots, or the faithful of the vicinity, let them

prevent the success of this conspiracy of the wicked, and set a worthy steward over *the house of God. (Rule* 31, 53, 64)

Obviously Benedict did not believe that God could be shut into a monastery as if he were not present everywhere, but there are degrees and modes of presence; Christ promised to be present in a special way (particularly to answer our prayers) "wherever two or three are gathered in my name" (Mt 18:19-20), and it is Benedict's desire that we live in our home and in our work-place in a way appropriate to recognition of God's presence and help our companions to be aware of it. That is how a human construction can become a "house of God." Not as if you could "make God present"; *he* is *our* Creator, not the other way round. But we can make ourselves aware of what is already here and who he is. Benedict was less impressed by Acts 17:24 ("God who made the world and everything in it, is Lord of heaven and earth and does not live in man-made temples") than by other verses of scripture. It is easy to sense the Creator's presence on an uninhabited island, in a forest, or on a mountain-top; Benedict wants us to reproduce their peace and quiet; it is undeniable that we can do the opposite with our noise and with sights as well as sounds; our words, spoken or written (e.g., "graffiti") and the decoration of our streets and homes, can "drive God away," in the sense that they replace our awareness of his presence with idols or distract us with unholy fantasies and ideas. (Iconography is the Church's weapon in response to pornography, the devil's weapon.)

God As Judge

God is our judge, whose judgment is present in a way analogous to a teacher's in his school, as the shepherd's to his sheep, as the parents' to their children; one might add, as the umpire's judgment (and even to the coach's and the scorekeeper's) at a game.

> Let the abbot always bear in mind that at the dread Judgment of God there will be an examination of these two matters: his teaching and the obedience of his disciples. . . . If the shepherd has bestowed all his pastoral diligence on a restless, unruly flock and tried every remedy for their unhealthy behavior, then he will be acquitted at the Lord's Judgment. . . . Let him know that he who has undertaken the

government of souls must prepare himself . . . he may be sure beyond doubt that on Judgment Day he will have to give the Lord an account of all these souls, as well as of his own. . . . He will have to render an account of all his decisions to God, the most just Judge. . . . Yet the abbot must not, by an arbitrary use of his power, ordain anything unjustly; but let him always think of the account he will have to render to God for all his decisions and his deeds. (*Rule* 2, 3, 63)

This severe warning to the abbot, to dread the Last Judgment, is nothing compared to the severity with which Benedict anticipates, as it were, God's judgment on "a detestable kind of monks" which he calls Sarabaites.

These, not having been tested, as gold in the furnace, by any rule or by the lessons of experience, are as soft as lead. In their works they still keep faith to the world, so that their tonsure marks them as liars before God.[1] They live in twos or threes, or even singly, without a shepherd, in their own sheepfolds and not in the Lord's. Their law is the desire for self-gratification: whatever enters their mind or appeals to them, that they call holy; what they dislike, they regard as unlawful. (*Rule* 1)

Evidently they have not reached the second degree of humility: "to love not one's own will nor take pleasure in satisfying one's desires."

"To fear the Day of Judgment" is among the Instruments of Good Works, which he calls "the tools of the spiritual craft. If we employ them unceasingly day and night and return them on the Day of Judgment, our compensation from the Lord will be that wage he has promised: 'Eye has not seen . . . what God has prepared for those who love him' " (*Rule* 4). At the twelfth degree of humility "he should consider himself already present at the dread Judgment and constantly say in his heart what the publican in the gospel said with his eyes fixed on the earth" (*Rule* 7). At the Work of God "let us therefore bring our tribute of praise to our Creator 'for the judgments of his justice' " (*Rule* 16). Of the Cellarer of the monastery (the person in charge of all the monastery's material goods): "Let him take the greatest care of the sick, of children, of guests and of the poor, knowing without doubt that he will have to render an account for all these on the Day of Judgment" (*Rule* 31).

---

1. Benedict detests lying and dishonesty, especially toward God.

As teachers test their students to see what they have learned, whether they are ready or not for promotion; as a pilot tests a new model of aircraft, to see if it can perform as designed; or as you simply test the air pressure in a tire, to see if it is safe for the road, so God too puts our souls through tests:

> In another place the scripture says, "You have tested us, O God; you have tried us as silver is tried by fire; you have brought us into a snare; you have laid afflictions on our back. . . . You have set men over our heads." (*Rule* 7)

But all this is because he loves us:

> Secure in their hope of a divine recompense, they go on with joy to declare, "but in all these trials we conquer, through him who has granted us his love. . . ." What can be sweeter to us, dear brethren, than this voice of the Lord inviting us? Behold, in his loving kindness the Lord shows us the way of life. (*Rule* 7 and Prol.)

He only loves the work of those who take their tests without hesitation or grumbling:

> The disciples should offer their obedience with a good will, for "God loves a cheerful giver." (*Rule* 5)

It is possible to please God:

> This very obedience will be acceptable to God . . . only if what is commanded is done without hesitation, delay, lukewarmness, grumbling, or objection. For the obedience given to superiors is given to God, since he himself has said, "He who hears you, hears me. . . ." If the disciple obeys with an ill-will and murmurs, not necessarily with his lips but simply in his heart, then even though he fulfill the command yet his work will not be acceptable to God, who sees that his heart is murmuring. (*Rule* 5)

Not even God likes a grouch. No one enjoys taking his dog for a walk, no matter how lovely the weather and the scenery, if it has to be dragged along unwillingly on its leash.

God's love is protective, and he helps us to pass the very tests he sets:

> Whoever you are, who are hastening to the heavenly homeland, fulfill *with the help of Christ* this minimum Rule which we have

written for beginners; and then at length *under God's protection*
you will attain to the loftier heights of doctrine and virtue. *(Rule* 73)

On the basis of this belief in God's good will, one must

put one's hope in God, [and] a brother commanded to do impossible
things is to know that this is for his good and obey out of love,
trusting in the help of God. *(Rule* 4 and 68)

The fact that God is judging us on the doing of his will, assumes that the
quality of our lives depends on the keeping of his commandments. The
sixty-second of the Instruments of Good Works is "to fulfill God's commandments daily in one's deeds," and the first degree of humility includes
"being ever mindful of all that God has commanded." Then:

If the community is a large one, let there be chosen out of it
brethren of good repute and holy life, and let them be appointed
deans. These shall take charge of their deaneries in all things,
observing the commandments of God and the instructions of their
abbot. Let men of such character be chosen deans that the abbot may
with confidence share his burdens among them. Let them be chosen
. . . according to their worthiness of life and the wisdom of their
doctrine. *(Rule* 21)

The criterion for classifying people as "of good repute and holy life" (or
worthiness of life), and "of such character that the abbot may with confidence
share his burdens with them," is primarily that they "observe the commandments of God" (and the instructions of their abbot, assuming that the two
coincide). It is our correspondence with God's commandments that deter-
mines our character. It is hoped that there will be some who will meet this
standard and be able to help others do the same.

If God is pleased with us, Benedict believes that "our compensation from
the Lord will be that wage he has promised: 'Eye has not seen,' etc." God is
expected to reward humility with the solace of a motherly kind of love, letting
us, like babies, feel the warmth of his heart: "Rather have I been of humble
mind than exalting myself; as a weaned child on its mother's breast, so you
solace my soul." It is right to hope for this, for

Scripture says, "He who perseveres to the end, he shall be saved."
[So], "Let your heart take courage and wait for the Lord!" Those

who are faithful . . . secure in their hope of a divine recompense, go on with joy to declare, "But in all these trials we conquer, through him who has granted us his love." (*Rule* 7)

But elsewhere Benedict warns the abbot that he must be fair in " 'making distribution to each according as anyone had need' (Acts 4:25); in all his decisions let [him] think about the retribution of God" (*Rule* 55), which rewards wrong decisions appropriately as well as right ones.

God Is Merciful

At the ceremonial reception of guests, when their hands and feet are washed by the abbot and community, "let them say this verse: 'We have received your mercy, O God, in the midst of your temple' " (*Rule* 53). Benedict wanted "all kindness to be shown" to guests; he would greet them with a reminder of God's mercy, rather than with a lecture on the Last Judgment. In the rather heavy prescription of confession, in the fifth degree of humility, he quotes the psalm, "Confess to the Lord," adding "for he is good, for his mercy endures forever" (*Rule* 7). A sense of God's mercy is at the root of what he means by motherly love. The last of the Instruments of Good Works is "never to despair of God's mercy." Not without this belief in God's mercy, one is advised by Benedict: "Daily in one's prayers, with tears and sighs, to confess one's past sins to God, and to amend them for the future," and "to make due satisfaction to God in the oratory" for such faults as being responsible for the monks rising so late that the Night Office has to be shortened (*Rule* 4 and 11).

God's mercy is shown equally to all, "for with God there is no respect of persons. Only for one reason are we preferred in his sight: if we be found better than others in good works and humility." God is fair. "Whether slaves or freemen, we are all one in Christ and bear an equal burden of service in the army of the same Lord." That is why "the abbot should show equal love to all and impose the same discipline on all according to their deserts, making no distinction of persons" (*Rule* 2).

God As King and Teacher

One comes to Benedict in order to

> renounce our own will to do battle under the Lord Christ, the true
> King. . . . Thus, never departing from his school but persevering in
> the monastery according to his teaching until death, we may by
> patience share in the sufferings of Christ and deserve to have a share
> also in his kingdom. (*Rule*, Prol.)

Of monks from other monasteries, he says:

> In every place it is the same Lord who is served, the same King
> for whom the battle is fought. . . . Having our loins girded, therefore,
> with faith and the performance of good works, let us walk in his
> paths by the guidance of the gospel, that we may deserve to see him
> who has called us to his kingdom. For if we wish to dwell in the tent
> of that kingdom, we must run to it by good deeds or we shall never
> reach it. . . . [Let the abbot] remember what is written: "First seek
> the kingdom of God and his justice." (*Rule* 61, Prol., 2)

Lumen Gentium, the Dogmatic Constitution of Vatican II "On the
Church" also speaks to religious of "their duty of working to implant and
strengthen the kingdom of Christ in souls and to extend that kingdom to every
land" (#44).

Where is this realm where God is King, this kingdom into which God has
called us? Does the fact that the abbot himself is called to seek it not assume
that it has not yet been found, even by him? Or does it assume that, by his
teaching and example, he can bring it about even in this life? If we are running
to that tent under the guidance of the gospel, that we may deserve to see God,
does that not assume that we do not dwell there now and cannot see him yet,
even if we dwell in "the house of God"?

God's kingdom cannot be located exactly in space and time, as on a map.
Yet, paradoxically, it is not absent from all space and time. When asked by
the Pharisees when it will come, our Lord replied: "You cannot tell by careful
watching. . . . Neither is it a matter of reporting that it is 'here' or 'there.' The
kingdom of God is already in your midst. . . . Wherever the carcass is, there
will the vultures gather" (Lk 17:20-21, 37), which seems to be a way of saying
it is wherever Jesus is, among people who believe in him. So it belongs to

the spiritual realm; it is a state of being, not a place. But its eternal, spiritual reality can be brought into this world ("If I cast out devils by the finger of God, then the kingdom of God is upon you," Lk 11:20). Benedict seems to have thought a monastic community the most likely kind of society to succeed in bringing it about. He would not deny that it can reign in a family; but it is most unlikely in an entire city or country. Insofar as it is almost synonymous with the Church, its relation to the world is set forth in two "Constitutions" of Vatican II, "On the Church" and "On the Church in the Modern World" (*Lumen Gentium* and *Gaudium et Spes*) with which modern Christians ought to be familiar. Suffice it to quote *Gaudium et Spes* here: "That the earthly and the heavenly city penetrate each other is a fact. . . . It remains a mystery of human history, which sin will keep in great disarray until the splendor of God's sons is fully revealed" (#40).

Benedict certainly hopes that the heavenly city has a foothold, so to speak, or an outpost in his monastery, where the Rule assumes battle to be in progress between God and the world. The latter are not opposed, as if God and his creation were by nature in conflict, but infinitely distinct as the Uncreated Being is distinct from his creation, and only when the Artist's intention is perfectly achieved will the prayer "thy kingdom come" be fully answered. It was Adam's duty (cf. Gn 1:28) to bring the created being into conformity with the Creator's plan: only so will the Artist's work be made perfect or nature be in harmony with its own internal laws, whose origin is in their First Cause.

Ever since the rebellion of the human creature started, the root of the battle is not between individuals belonging to one army or the other but within each individual's soul. Nevertheless it is usual that people of property and power, engaged in commerce, politics and war, belong to "the world" of enmity toward God and his Christ, under the influence of unholy spirits. (In the modern world, the Italian stigmatic Padre Pio thought the media, at least television, was possessed by the devil.) And monks belong to God, owing allegiance to him as their King. But monks *can* become worldly; indeed, if they are not perfectly humble, they have a bit of the world in them. And kings, queens, businessmen, soldiers, and lawyers have often been good Christians and even become saints, as totally dedicated to God and his kingdom as a monk or nun should be. History has many examples of each, Giorgio LaPira, for one, a mayor of Florence (Italy) in the middle of the twentieth century, a good candidate for beatification and an agent of God's kingdom in "the world." And Thomas More in the past, not to mention a number of queens, like Saint Margaret, who loved the Benedictines and brought them to Scotland in the eleventh century. She was buried at their Abbey.

The distinction between "the world" and "the Church" can be illusory on the local level. The rival kingdoms have agents in each other's camp who can gain control. The distinction is not the same as the distinction between Church and state. Benedict would have no quarrel with their separation as a general principle. It would be absurd to think of his approving of a state which defined itself as militantly atheistic, but neither would he think the exclusion of ecclesiastics and monks from political office a bad idea. On the contrary, union of Church and state in the sense of making membership in the Church a requirement for political office can get the Church blamed for crimes committed by officials whose lives belie their allegiance to Christ; and making abbots or bishops civil rulers, opens the door to men entering monasteries or the clergy in order to achieve political ambitions, with disastrous results for a monastery or the Church. At one crazy time in the Middle Ages, for instance, the abbot of Subiaco was at war with the pope, each leading men under arms against the other.

We spoke of the world and the Church or monastery as rival camps; we mentioned ways in which a worldly person, an agent of the world as it were, might enter a monastery; Satan can also infiltrate and strangle a monastery by making it economically dependent on servants of Mammon (money, cf. Lk 16:13) or of the state, who use its resources for their own ends rather than God's. Benedict is aware that Satan will try to infiltrate even into the abbot himself, not without possible success.

This seeming digression was necessary to explain the following quotations implying an opposition between God and the world: in chapter 1 "On the Kinds of Monks" he describes Sarabaites, "a detestable kind of monks, still *loyal to the world* by their actions." One of the Instruments of Good Works is "to become a stranger to the world's ways." And he says, in chapter 64, that "whether the work which the abbot enjoins *concerns God or the world*, let him be discreet and moderate." In the chapter "On Brethren Who Are Sent On a Journey" he says:

> When brethren return from a journey . . . let them lie prostrate on the floor of the oratory and beg the prayers of all on account of any faults that may have surprised them on the road, through the seeing or hearing of something evil, or through idle talk. And let no

one presume to tell another whatever he may have seen or heard outside of the monastery, because this causes very great harm. (*Rule* 67)

In other words, he did not expect monks when outside the monastery (in the world of his time) to escape temptation in the form of something which might distract their hearts from total dedication to God. He did not expect them to be able to see or hear anything which could help their brethren either, in the battle for Christ their King. In the 1980's, a deeply religious person said she preferred to close her eyes when she was driven through Rome now; but she loved it when she lived there nearly half a century ago; it now displays too much of "the world."

With his invitation to "seek the kingdom of God, so that you may deserve to see him who has called us to his kingdom," Benedict is not promising that we shall find God's kingdom in any stable, secure sense in a monastery, or have the face-to-face vision of God in this life. We are not yet in his kingdom. But we choose to belong to Christ as our King. When we suffer with him, we are sharing in his battle to establish his kingdom (primarily right here in our own hearts that we want to make his). We choose to help him and count on his help to win possession of the kingdom that is rightfully his and that he desires. ("Whoever you are, therefore, who are hastening to the heavenly homeland, fulfill *with the help of Christ* this minimum Rule.") This will lead to seeing God, if you persevere. Something more, however, than "pie in the sky when you die"; as we have already seen, some solace will be offered along the way, Christ present among his troops; so long as you are faithfully trying to stay in his school and to learn the spiritual craft, by that very faith you will know he is with you. You may not see him, but you can hear his voice and be taught by his word in the liturgy, in your heart, or in your reading, and he does give us his lights:

> Let us open our eyes to the deifying light. . . . Run while you have the light of life, lest the darkness of death overtake you. Let us hear with attentive ears the warning which the divine voice cries daily to us, "Today if you hear his voice, harden not your hearts." And again, "He who has ears to hear, let him hear what the Spirit says to the churches." And what does he say? "Come, my children, listen to me, I will teach you the fear of the Lord." And the Lord, seeking his laborer in the multitude to whom he thus cries out, says

again, "Who is the man who will have life, and desires to see good days?"... What can be sweeter to us, dear brethren, than this voice of the Lord inviting us? Behold, in his loving kindness the Lord shows us the way of life. (*Rule*, Prol.)

God's voice is recognized by Benedict as the voice of loving kindness and is responded to with our own love.

With Christ as our master, "never departing from his school, we now share in his sufferings" (which can be terrible), "so that [later] we may deserve to have a share also in his kingdom." "To share in his sufferings" is an aspect of "doing battle under the Lord Christ, the true King." If we hear his voice as the master in our school, the master also of suffering well, we know by faith that he is present in some mysterious way.

Benedict's faith sees Christ present in many ways:

> *The abbot* is believed to hold the place of Christ in the monastery. He is to be called "Lord" and "abbot," not for any claim of his own but out of honor and love for Christ. He, for his part, must reflect on this and in his behavior show himself worthy of such honor. (*Rule* 63)
>
> Before all things and above all things, care must be taken of *the sick*, so that they will be served as if they were Christ in person; for he himself said, "I was sick, and you visited me." All *guests* who present themselves are to be welcomed as Christ, for he himself will say: "I was a stranger and you welcomed me." (*Rule* 36 and 53)

In an article on the "Ecclesial Nature of Benedictine Spirituality," in the 5 August 1992 issue of the Weekly Edition in English of the *Osservatore Romano*, Mariano Dell'Omo refers to hospitality as "the litmus test of a monastic community," and an instance of how truly "Benedict decidedly excludes a monastic asceticism which could be translated into disdain for the world."

> Proper honor must be shown to all, especially to those who share our faith and to pilgrims. In the salutation of all guests, whether arriving or departing, let all humility be shown. Let the head be bowed or the whole body prostrated on the ground in adoration of Christ, who indeed is received in their persons. Great care and concern are to be shown in receiving poor people and pilgrims,

because in them more particularly Christ is received; our very awe of the rich guarantees them special respect. (*Rule* 53)

But it is not only outside of us, in our neighbor, that God is present:

> The Lord calls out, "Is there anyone here who yearns for life, and desires to see good days?" And if, hearing him, you answer, "I do," God says to you, "If you will have true and everlasting life. . . . Turn away from evil and do good; seek after peace and pursue it. And when you have done these things, my eyes shall be upon you and my ears open to your prayers; and before you call upon me, I will say to you, 'Behold, here I am.' " (*Rule*, Prol.)

God makes his presence felt to those who turn away from evil and do good, who seek peace and life and "good days"; they know they can turn to him as a friend.

The negative side of the honor, love, adoration, and service of Christ is to deny your own will in order to do his:

> To you, therefore, my words are now addressed, whoever you may be, who are renouncing your own will to do battle under the Lord Christ, the true King, and are taking up the strong, bright weapons of obedience. (*Rule*, Prol.)[1]

Obedience only makes sense as a way of loving God. The tenth Instrument of Good Works is "to deny oneself in order to follow Christ," wherever one hears his voice or recognizes his word and his will. The abbot himself must be obedient to God:

> Lest God one day say to him in his sin, "Why do you declare my statutes and profess my covenant with your lips, whereas you hate discipline and have cast my words behind you?" . . . Let [the abbot] fear the prophet's warning through which God says, "What you saw to be fat you took to yourselves, and what was feeble you cast away." Let him rather imitate the loving example of the Good Shepherd. (*Rule* 2 and 27)

---

1. The reader may review here what was quoted on pp. 54-56, concerning obedience, "which comes naturally to those who cherish Christ above all. . . . They carry out the superior's order as if the command came from God himself. . . . To teachers the Lord says, 'Whoever hears you, hears me.' "

We have seen in the first degree of humility that

> truly, we are forbidden to do our own will, for scripture tells us: "Turn away from your desires." And in the [Lord's] Prayer too we ask God that his will be done in us. We are rightly taught not to do our own will, since we dread what scripture says: "There are ways which men call right that in the end plunge into the depths of hell." Moreover, we fear what is said of those who ignore this: "They are corrupt and have become depraved in their desires." (*Rule* 7)

God Our Father and Lord

God is to be served as our Lord and loved as our Father:

> You have received a Spirit of adoption as sons, by virtue of which we cry, "Abba—Father!" We must always so serve him with the good things he has given us, that he will never as an angry Father disinherit his children, nor ever as a dread Lord, provoked by our evil actions, deliver us to everlasting punishment as wicked servants who would not follow him to glory. (*Rule* 2 and Prol.)

Recall again the first degree of humility, which is

> that a man keeps the fear of God always before his eyes and never forgets it. He must constantly remember everything God has commanded, keeping in mind that all who despise God will burn in hell for their sins, and all who fear God have everlasting life awaiting them. (*Rule* 7)

The Rule reveals Benedict as a gentle and compassionate person, but he could thunder when it was appropriate.

The Object of Worship and Sacrifice

God is also the object of sacrifice; a way to express our devotion to him is to make sacrifices:

> During these days [of Lent], therefore, let us increase somewhat the usual burden of our service, as by private prayers and by

abstinence in food and drink. Thus everyone of his own will may offer God "with joy of the Holy Spirit" something above the measure required of him. (*Rule* 49)

If anyone of the nobility offers his son to God in the monastery and the boy is very young, let his parents draw up the petition which we mentioned above; and at the presentation of the gifts [presumably at the eucharist] let them wrap the petition and the boy's hand in the altar cloth and so offer him. (*Rule* 59)

God is to be honored also in the service of people, as we have seen in the service of the sick:

Let the sick on their part consider that they are being served *for the honor of God*. [Therefore], for these sick brethren let there be assigned a special room and an attendant who is *God-fearing*, diligent and solicitous. (*Rule* 36)

God's special presence in the oratory is to be honored by reverence:

Let the oratory be a place of prayer. When the Work of God is ended, let all go out in perfect silence, and let reverence for God be observed. (*Rule* 52)

Giver of Grace and of All Good, and of Nothing But Good

Since all good comes from God, obviously we owe him thanks, which can be expressed in simple ways:

Let us follow the scripture, "Distribution was made to each according as anyone had need." He who needs less *should thank God* and not be discontented. (*Rule* 34)

We thank God for his gifts, including the gift of being able to get along on less than other people.

At the gate of the monastery let there be placed a wise old man, so that those who come may always find someone at hand. As soon as anyone knocks or a poor man hails him, let him answer "Thanks be to God!" (*Rule* 66)

Under all circumstances, God is to be praised, blessed, and glorified. This is given expression especially in public worship and common prayer; at the end of the Night Office on Sundays, before the reading of the gospel for the day, "let the abbot begin the hymn 'We praise you, O God' " (the *Te Deum,* an ancient Latin hymn). The brethren should take turns serving one another from the kitchen, a week at a time:

> Immediately after the Morning Office on Sunday, the incoming and outgoing servers shall prostrate themselves before all the brethren in the oratory and ask their prayers. Let the server who is ending his week say this verse: "*Blessed are you, O Lord God, who have helped me and consoled me*" *(Rule* 35),

recognizing not only that we are serving God when we serve one another at table, but we cannot do even this without God's aid. In granting permission for monks to drink wine with their meals, if God has not given them the strength to abstain, Benedict quotes the scripture:

> "Everyone has his own gift from God, one in this way and another in that. . . ." But where the circumstances of the place are such that not even the measure prescribed above can be supplied, but much less or none at all, *let those who live there bless God* and not murmur. (*Rule* 40)

The reason why avarice is not to creep into the prices for goods produced by the monastery's craftsmen, "but the goods are always to be sold a little cheaper than they can be sold by people in the world," is "that in all things God may be glorified" (*Rule* 57). The way we live, even the way we do business, can contribute to the honor or dishonor of God.

Benedict is convinced that any good in us is thanks to the grace of God (the "uncreated energy" of the Holy Spirit, according to the terminology common in Eastern monastic circles). Benedictine life would be impossible without grace; it might be described as the life of God living in human beings who cooperate with it; therefore

> those who [fearing the Lord] do not pride themselves on their good observance, are convinced that the good which is in them cannot come from themselves and must be from the Lord. They glorify the Lord's work in them, using the words of the prophet, "not to us, O Lord, not to us, but to your name give the glory." Thus also the

apostle Paul attributed nothing of the success of his preaching to himself but said, "By the grace of God I am what I am." And again he says, "He who glories, let him glory in the Lord." (*Rule*, Prol.)

The senior assigned to watch over the novices is "to test the spirits to see whether they are from God." "To test the spirits," in this context, means discerning that a person's desire to enter the monastery is a free response to the working grace, the Spirit of God. It is because of the indispensable need of grace that it was said in the Prologue: "Whatever good work you begin to do, beg of him with most earnest prayer to perfect it." And every Office begins with the prayer: "God, come to my assistance; O Lord, make haste to help me," which was the verse Cassian says the Desert Fathers would repeat to themselves, as later the monks of the East repeated the "Jesus Prayer." Trusting absolutely in the willingness of God to give us this grace according to our need, an Instrument of Good Works is "to put one's hope in God," and "the brother commanded to do impossible things is to obey out of love, trusting in the help of God." "The living God" is not living just apart in heaven but in his Church, his children, and must be found there and in our own souls.

Benedict does not advise living as a hermit, except "after long probation in a monastery"; to live a religious life, one needs the help of many brethren as well as the grace of God (perhaps he learned this from the hardships of his own beginning).

> Hermits are those who, no longer in the first fervor of their reformation but after long probation in a monastery, having learned by the help of many brethren how to fight against the devil, go out well armed from the ranks of the community to the solitary combat of the desert. They are able now, *with no help save from God*, to fight single-handed against the vices of the flesh and their own evil thoughts. (*Rule* 1)

They are still not able to do it alone without the grace of God.

Besides weekly "kitcheners" who wait on tables, one monk is to read to the rest while they take their meals in silence:

> The meals of the brethren should not be without reading. Let this incoming reader, after Mass and communion, ask all to pray for him that God may keep him from the spirit of pride. (*Rule* 38)

An acknowledgement that one needs the prayers of the brethren, because without grace one cannot be free of pride.

The Goal of Human Life and Object of All Our Love

Human life has a goal: the vision of God and eternal union with him. Therefore it is a journey of discovery and a search (by the labor of obedience) "to return to him from whom you had departed by the sloth of disobedience. . . . It is love that impels them to pursue everlasting life. That desire is their motive for choosing the narrow way" of obedience to another's command, "which leads to life" (*Rule*, Prol. and 5). The journey is not started without some understanding of what (or whom) you seek:

> At all times "the Lord looks down from heaven on the sons of men to see whether any *understand* and seek God." The senior assigned to watch over the novices with the utmost care [must] examine whether the novice *is truly seeking God* and whether he is zealous for the Work of God, for obedience and for humiliations. The novice should be told all the hard and rugged ways by which *the journey to God* is made. . . . Not only is obedience a blessing to be shown by all to the abbot, but the brethren are also to obey one another, knowing that *by this road of obedience they are going to God.* (*Rule* 7, 58, 71)

Obedience is a good thing in itself, but it acquires the most value when it is used as a road to God. "As we progress in this way of life and in faith," which implies also "in understanding," "our hearts expand and we run the way of God's commandments with the inexpressible delight of love" (*Rule*, Prol.).

In a sense, the love of God is both the end of the spiritual life and its beginning: "*In the first place,* to love the Lord God with the whole heart, the whole soul, the whole strength" is number one among the Instruments of Good Works. It is to give God his due. " The third degree of humility is that a person *for the love of God* submit himself to his superior in all obedience" (*Rule* 7), "which is the virtue of those who hold nothing dearer to them than Christ" (*Rule* 5). "Let them prefer nothing whatever to Christ" (*Rule* 72). "To prefer nothing to the love of Christ" is another of the Instruments of Good Works. The second degree of humility is "that a person love not his own will . . . but model his actions on the saying of the Lord, 'I have come not to do my own will, but the will of him who sent me' " (*Rule* 7). What gives greater value to the renunciation of self-love and represents progress in humility, is that the energy of love is directed away from self toward God and Christ, as one struggles up the remaining steps. As we saw in the Introduction, this love is tempered with a certain fear of God and dread of his judgment.

> Having climbed all the steps of humility, the monk will quickly arrive at that *perfect love of God* which casts out fear. And all those precepts which formerly he had not observed without fear, he will now begin to keep by reason of that love, without any effort, as though naturally and by habit. No longer will his motive be the fear of hell but rather *the love of Christ*, good habit and delight in the virtues which the Lord will deign to show forth by the Holy Spirit in his servant now cleansed from vice and sin. (*Rule* 7)

This is the culmination of the work of the Holy Spirit, the establishment of the kingdom of God in the soul, the final victory in the "battle under the Lord Christ, the true King," which is assumed to be the point at which Benedict arrived, or he could not have written of it. This is the way he felt about the God who was the object of his prayer, "the Lord God of the universe, before whom it is necessary to lay our petitions with complete humility and sincere devotion" (*Rule* 20). God is the Being eminently worthy of human love, second to whom, and for whose sake, all human beings deserve our love. Having arrived at such love and knowledge of God, he could not but give primacy of place to "the Work of God": "Let nothing, therefore, be put before the Work of God." It is never to be neglected, even by monks who cannot get to the oratory, as we have seen in the chapter on Prayer. "To pray for one's enemies in the love of Christ" is another of Benedict's instructions on prayer among the Instruments of Good Works. No one is to be excluded from one's prayer, as no one is excluded from Christ's love. It is this love of Christ which is the motive for what Benedict twice says about the way to deal with temptations and evil thoughts:

> "Lord, who shall dwell in your tent, or who shall rest upon your holy mountain?" . . . It is he who has laid hold of his thoughts while they were still young and dashed them against Christ. (*Rule*, Prol. and 4)

"Whether slave or free, we are all One in Christ," that is why the abbot should avoid any favoritism. Christ is the person Benedict loves, and loving him only, "he shows equal love to all, unless he finds someone better than another in good works and in humility" (because in such a one Christ is more present).

God as "described" in the Rule of Benedict is evidently God as Benedict has experienced him in the spiritual life—presupposing the meditation of God's Word—rather than as he can be known by logical reasoning and metaphysical speculation.

We can see his theology as the basis of the way of life he teaches, conditioned by his experience as the spiritual father of many disciples in a time and place distant from our own. Were you to read a biography of some recently canonized saint from relatively modern times, curious to see what they may have emphasized in conditions more similar to our own, there would probably be nuances of their faith in God which, without conflicting with Benedict's, would flow from other words of Christ in response to different needs than those which are prominent in Benedict's Rule. Picking two at random: John Neumann as bishop of Philadelphia (and all that led up to that) in the middle of the nineteenth century, had a different call from Benedict's, and different needs to care for in the faithful he served as a missionary; Jeanne Jugan as a Breton peasant, foundress of the Little Sisters of the Poor, at roughly the same distance in time from Benedict, had yet another call and another vision, perhaps too simple to be the object of an essay like this but nonetheless a powerful influence for good, long beyond her lifetime, similar to Benedict at least in her humility.

New City Press has published just such a study of God in the experience and thought of a contemporary writer, Chiara Lubich: *God Who Is Love*, by Marisa Cerini.[1] Lubich's experience issues from the Second World War. She is a woman, highly educated especially in philosophy, who is not called to monastic life but to be a guide for others, lay people in particular. So, naturally her unique life and thought differs from Benedict's; if Benedict emphasizes more the *fear* of God's *Judgment*, remember that he was writing for beginners, many of whom would be very young, or very ignorant, or could have come to him immediately out of a very sinful or barbarous life. Types like that need to be reminded of judgment, as the psalms say: "the fear of the

---

1. Marisa Cerini, *God Who Is Love* (New York: New City Press, 1992).

Lord is the beginning of wisdom," wisdom being more or less synonymous with sanctity.

We might add as a postscript that the study of what God meant even to agnostics or atheists can tell us much, not only about them but also about the influence they have had. If they rejected the idea of God, we may say that we too do not believe in what they define as God; and we realize the importance for ourselves of getting the right idea from those who knew him best (the saints). Not to know God is, after all, a sin, a very serious one; "the greatest sin of modern times, my brothers, is ignorance," said a popular preacher in 1986.

Community Life

If we are to be protected from the distractions and allurements of the world, something positive has to be done to occupy our interest and our time in a way that will develop our relationship with God and keep us from idleness or getting bored. Having prescribed a certain number of hours of the day and night for prayer in his attempt to organize a viable community life under the guidance of the gospel, Benedict divides the rest of the day between sacred reading and manual labor. "From the Rule's forty-eighth chapter which deals specifically with the question of manual labor, as well as from other references to field work, it is clear where Benedict's preference lay. The work most suitable for monks was, in relation to the other aspects of his idea, farm or agricultural labor."[1]

Community Property, the Locus of Community Life

Another aspect of the life of a community is its property. The view of the Bible and of early Christianity is that everything in God's creation is good, belongs to him, and can be useful for our "return to him from whom we had departed by the sloth of disobedience" (*Rule,* Prol.). Temporal and material things are no exception. But sin can disfigure their beauty or divert them from their purpose.[2]

Like any human society which needs to be self-supporting and self-contained, a monastery has to have its own buildings and land; Benedict considers them sacred to God and allows individuals to own none of them; not even the abbot or the Cellarer; God is the owner of this land and of everything in it. The desire for ownership is another of the desires that has to be mortified (cf. the second degree of humility, p. 67 above).

---

1. Dom Hubert van Zeller, *The Benedictine Idea* (London: Burns and Oates, 1959), p. 45. This highly readable, excellent outline of Benedictinism in its historical development, is well worth obtaining and reading.
2. Cf. *The Rule of St. Benedict in Latin and English with Notes* (Collegeville: The Liturgical Press, 1981), p. 370.

> If it can be done, the monastery should be so constructed that all
> the necessary things, such as water, mill, garden and various work-
> shops, may be within the enclosure. Then there will be no need for
> the monks to roam outside, since that is not at all profitable for their
> souls. . . . Let the Cellarer regard all the utensils of the monastery
> and its whole property as if they were the sacred vessels of the altar.
> (*Rule* 66 and 31)

Land which has been the site of a monastery for centuries noticeably
retains an aura of hallowed ground, though it has subsequently passed into
secular hands.

We have seen (on p. 70), in connection with the sale of the monastery's
goods, that Benedict was aware that "the sin of avarice can creep in": greed
for more property or, one might add, the possessiveness of holding on to what
has been acquired in excess of what is needed. As is well known from history,
Benedict's pragmatic wisdom was so successful economically that it aroused
the world's envy. Because of the very success of the Rule of Benedict from
an economic, political point of view, secular powers have tried to control
monasteries for their own interests, and monks have found themselves
virtually their slaves. Tyrannical kings confiscated monastic land to enrich
themselves and solidify their power. But many monasteries, which built or
acquired what they needed for a community of two or three hundred people,
or even thousands, held on to land they did not need when their numbers
dwindled, which invites confiscation; the poor, often well taken care of by
the monks, were not the ones to benefit; even three-and-a-half centuries after
the dissolution of Glastonbury Abbey in the West of England, farmers were
heard saying, "It's too bad they turned the monks out." They felt their
forebears, as tenants of a monastery, got a better deal.

When a novice at the end of his probationary period decides to take
monastic vows, "If he has any property," Benedict says,

> let him either give it beforehand to the poor or by solemn donation
> bestow it on the monastery, reserving nothing at all for himself, as
> indeed he knows that from that day forward he will not even have
> his own body at his disposal. *He is then* divested of his own clothes
> and dressed in the clothes of the monastery. But let the clothes of
> which he was divested be put aside in the wardrobe and kept there.
> Then if he should ever listen to the persuasions of the devil and

decide to leave the monastery (which God forbid), he may be divested of the monastic clothes and cast out. (*Rule* 58)

One senses the sadness felt by Benedict if a brother left. Of the taking of vows, he says,

he who is to be received shall make a promise before all in the oratory. This promise he shall make before God and his saints, so that if he should ever act otherwise, he may know that he will be condemned by him whom he mocks. (*Rule* 58)

Mention was made on page 128 of an ancient practice, whereby a nobleman

offers his son to God in the monastery: As regards their property, they shall promise in the same petition under oath that they will never of themselves, or through an intermediary, or in any way whatever, give him anything or provide him with the opportunity of owning anything. Or else, if they are unwilling to do this, and if they want to offer something as an alms to the monastery for their advantage, let them make a donation of the property to the monastery, reserving the income to themselves if they wish. And in this way let everything be barred, so that the boy may have no expectations whereby (which God forbid) he might be deceived and ruined, as we have learned by experience. (*Rule* 59)

Benedict has no illusions that it could be quite a temptation to a monk to accept an unexpected legacy; and he has been saddened when it could not be prevented. Evidently he has seen souls ruined by wealth. After Eastern Europe joined the "free world," at least one of his successors was deeply saddened to see young monks lured away, not by private legacies but by floods of licentious materials (illegal under Soviet rule) poured in from the affluent West. One is reminded of the story of the rich young man in the gospel (Mk 10:17-30); Benedict is saddened by awareness that as the rich young man "went away sad," so will the rich young monk, in the long run, if he leaves; possessions, not unlike licentiousness, are a deceptive path to happiness.

Benedict is very serious about the strict prohibition of any private property. "Beds, moreover, are to be examined frequently by the abbot, to see if any private property be found in them" (*Rule* 55). (They are the only place a monk could hide anything, since he had no private room.)

If anyone should be found to have something that he did not receive from the abbot, let him undergo the most severe discipline. And in order that this vice of private ownership may be cut out by the roots, the abbot should provide all the necessary articles . . . that all pretext of need may be taken away. (*Rule* 55)

This vice especially is to be cut out of the monastery by the roots. Let no one presume to give or receive anything without the abbot's leave, or to have anything as his own—anything whatever, whether book or tablets or pen or whatever it may be—since they are not permitted to have even their bodies or wills at their own disposal; but for all their necessities let them look to the Father of the monastery. And let it be unlawful to have anything which the abbot has not given or allowed. Let all things be common to all, as it is written, and let no one say or assume that anything is his own. (*Rule* 33)

Chapter 31 of the Rule is devoted to "What Kind of Man the Cellarer of the Monastery Should Be." There are sensitive points here which can be reflected upon by any Christian in the world who has to administer property: the manager of a business or a store, for instance, the quartermaster in the military, even a housewife. Let them be encouraged by Benedict's assurance that the performance of their duties also comes under the guidance of the gospel and can sanctify them. They can apply to themselves what can be said of monastic Cellarers: if they relate well to the people they serve and run the operation smoothly and efficiently, they contribute enormously to peace in the entire community. One has to give Benedict credit for much understanding of good business psychology, as well as of community sensitivities, in his instructions to the Cellarer.

As cellarer of the monastery let there be chosen from the community one who is wise, of mature character, sober, not a great eater, not haughty, not excitable, not offensive, not slow, not wasteful, but a God-fearing man who may be like a father to the whole community. (*Rule* 31)

"Wise": obviously one ought not to accept such heavy responsibility without the gift of practical wisdom: intelligence in seeing ways to use the resources at hand to produce income and ways to conserve resources and save money—hence: "not wasteful."

"Of mature character": a person who is immature may be unrealistic, a bit of a dreamer about possibilities, or may be so insecure as to be over-anxious to please everybody, whereas that cannot be done in an administrative post. "Not excitable" also is connected with maturity, not tending to panic when times are hard; in those days famines could strike and bad harvests due to weather conditions. An administrator has to be able to keep cool, and reassure the community with his optimism and confidence.

"Sober, not a great eater": the name Cellarer derives from his having access to as well as charge of the cellar, where wine barrels and food supplies are stored; so it is not a safe position for an alcoholic or a glutton, who would tend to be wasteful, to his own detriment as well as others'.

"Not haughty": the Latin word is *elatus*; this is a spiritual consideration; he should not get "elated" over the honor concomitant with the position, or his humility will suffer. "Not offensive" is connected with humility; he should not treat his brethren with contempt or rudeness, just because he is set over them in temporal matters, or he will be a great trial to them all.

"Not slow": again, it will be trying if he tests the brethren's patience by being slow over supplying their needs, coming across with them only at the last minute, or if they have to waste time pleading and arguing over reasonable requests.

"Being like a father": he does not give them life, as the abbot does in a spiritual sense, but he must try to inspire confidence as a good provider. These last four qualities have to do with what follows about "not vexing the brethren."

"Let him have charge of everything. He shall do nothing without the abbot's orders but keep to his instructions" (cf. p. 36 above, from *The Life and Miracles of Saint Benedict*, chapter 28).

> Let him not vex the brethren. If any brother happens to make some unreasonable demand of him, instead of vexing the brother with a contemptuous refusal, he should humbly give the reason for denying the improper request. (*Rule* 31)

These principles are an application of Benedict's doctrine on humility and obedience, but they show Benedict's sensitivity to how hard it could be for the Cellarer, should the latter be aware that he not only "has charge of everything," but may be a lot more knowledgeable about temporal matters than the abbot himself. Even though from an economic point of view the abbot could be wrong in some decision, the Cellarer is only his servant and must obey instructions, like a subordinate officer in the military, which may not be easy.

"To humbly give the reason for denying an improper request" is simply to treat his brethren respectfully as intelligent adults, or else they might become irrational; treating them like children does not help them mature; it is an act of pride to assume they cannot understand the reason for hard decisions. They share his need for concern for the matters over which he is their steward, the community's temporal well-being. To explain decisions could be very helpful to those who may later have to assume the present Cellarer's responsibilities.

"Let him keep guard over his own soul"—a special precaution to one who is still no less a monk, though his duties require him to give so much attention to material things (one recalls that the apostle who betrayed Jesus was the very one who was entrusted with the purse), "mindful always of the apostle's saying that 'he who has ministered well acquires for himself a good standing.' Let him take the greatest care of the sick, of children, of guests and of the poor, knowing without doubt that he will have to render an account for all these on the Day of Judgment"—a sensitive reminder of the particular responsibilities of the Cellarer, where general principles have already been forcibly laid down.

The care of material things can sanctify the Cellarer: "Let him regard all the utensils of the monastery and its whole property as if they were the sacred vessels of the altar. Let him not think that he may neglect anything. He should be neither a miser nor a prodigal and squanderer of the monastery's substance" (just like the father of a family has to beware of risky enterprises), "but should do all things with measure and in accordance with the abbot's instructions." What Benedict said to the abbot: "Do everything with counsel, and you will not repent when you have done it," would apply equally to the Cellarer.

"Above all things let him have humility" (Benedict has mentioned humility twice already, which shows he is conscious that the duties of Cellarer can be a dangerous occasion of pride); "and if he has nothing else to give let him give a good word in answer, for it is written, 'A good word is above the best gift'" (*Rule* 31). This too is a repetition of the admonition not to vex the brethren but to be humbly reasonable with them.

> Let him have under his care all that the abbot has assigned to him
> but not presume to deal with what he has forbidden him. Let him

give the brethren their appointed allowance of food without any arrogance or delay, that they may not be scandalized, mindful of the Word of God as to what he deserves "who shall scandalize one of the little ones." (*Rule* 31)

Benedict's repeated exhortation to obedience reflects a realization of the dangers inherent in the Cellarer's opportunities for acting independently, as though he owned the place. The word translated as "arrogance" is an uncommon one for pride, a Greek word (*typhos*) which basically means "smoke, mist, cloud"; Benedict might have in mind another danger, that the Cellarer operate behind a kind of smoke screen of secretiveness, concealing actual conditions or his operations from the community and even from the abbot; it can also mean "folly." The warning against giving scandal refers to how much the Cellarer can contribute, positively or negatively, to peace in the community.

But the poor Cellarer too needs to be able to live and work in peace, and without excessive trouble or vexation:

If the community is a large one, let helpers be given him, that by their assistance he may fulfill with a quiet mind the office committed to him. The proper times should be observed in giving the things that have to be given and asking for the things that have to be asked for, that no one may be troubled or vexed in the house of God. (*Rule* 31)

Enough has been quoted to make Benedict's mind clear on the subject of human relationships—an important consideration for personal growth in a community—about relations, for instance, with the abbot, the sick, with old men and boys (obviously the same applies to women and girls in convents), and with guests.

Manual Labor and Sacred Reading

Idleness is the enemy of the soul. Therefore the brethren should be occupied at certain times in manual labor and again at fixed hours in sacred reading. To that end . . . from Easter until the Calends of October [October 1] when they come out from Prime in the morning let them labor at whatever is necessary until about the fourth hour,

> and from the fourth hour until about the sixth let them apply
> themselves to reading. (*Rule* 48)

Remember that on the Roman "clock," the day is divided into twelve hours, so the sixth hour is always midday. Prime (the "first hour") is prayed about an hour after sunrise, and takes about a quarter of an hour. So they work three or four hours and then settle down to two hours of reading. This schedule is adapted to the oppressively hot summers in central Italy. You will find today that shops close from noon till 4 P.M.; practically everyone goes home for their main meal and takes it easy until the sun begins to decline.

As we have noted before, Benedict is realistic and adapts his schedule to the rhythms of nature as well as of the Christian liturgical year. He would have us do the same: not follow exactly the same schedule as he but adapt a life of prayer, work, and sacred reading to conditions where we live, which in today's high-tech society are not determined so much by the rhythms of nature (because we have artificial light, air conditioning, etc.). All that has been said, for instance by the "Greens" and about ecology and about the natural law, has made us aware that if our lives were closer to nature they might be better. Benedict would not disagree, but he would tell us to be realistic. (*He* did without all the uses of gas, electricity, and oil, or an elevator between floors, but how much can *you*, really?) Many of these things have become second nature and necessities, though we may be unnecessarily addicted to some.

> After the sixth hour, having left the table, let them rest on their beds
> in perfect silence; or if anyone may perhaps want to read, let him read
> to himself in such a way as not to disturb anyone else.[1] Let None[2] be
> said rather early, at the middle of the eighth hour [c. 2:30], and let
> them again do what work has to be done until Vespers. (*Rule* 48)

That means about three hours of work in the afternoon (starting an hour earlier than is considered bearable in a present-day Italian summer), or a total of seven hours of work and two hours of reading, or three if one read during the siesta period. Five or six hours a day would be devoted to prayer and reading, about the same amount of time as it is said the average person spends watching TV nowadays.

---

1. In the ancient world, it was usual to read aloud.
2. The prayers said at the ninth hour, c. 3 P.M.; Latin *Nona* = ninth.

One might ask whether watching religious programs on videos and television would be essentially the same as sacred reading. Not quite, because viewing television is passive; reading involves more mental activity and concentration; "sacred" reading is rather like a dialogue between the reader and the word of God. Using a tape deck when driving to and from work, however, is a way we can use technology to hear something of God, in words or in song. A Capuchin friar, already quoted before, told his congregation, "The modern world's greatest sin, my brothers, is ignorance." We do need to read, or inform ourselves the best way we can, about the things which matter most.

> And if the circumstances of the place or their poverty should require that they themselves do the work of gathering the harvest, let them not be discontented; for then are they truly monks when they live by the labor of their hands, as did our Fathers and the apostles. Let all things be done with moderation, however, for the sake of the fainthearted. (*Rule* 48)

It appears that Benedict did not disapprove of monks employing outside help for gathering the harvest, if they could afford it and were not very hardy themselves. But his ideal was that they do their own work; Benedict definitely thought there is spiritual value in manual labor. *Perfectae Caritatis* expresses Benedict's mind: "In discharging his duty, each religious should regard himself as subject to the common law of labor" (#13). His call for moderation shows his awareness of overwork's danger, not only to the health of the weak, but also to the proper balance between work and prayer/reading; the latter should not be neglected for the sake of economy or for any other reason; without it, the soul dies of malnutrition. *Perfectae Caritatis* #13 must be balanced by other principles enunciated in the same decree: "Drawing on the authentic sources of Christian spirituality, let the members of communities energetically cultivate the spirit of prayer and the practice of it. . . . Thus they are the glory of the Church and an overflowing fountain of heavenly graces" (#6 and #7).

> From the Calends of October until the beginning of Lent, let them apply themselves to reading up to the end of the second hour.[1] At the second hour let Terce[2] be said, and then let all labor at the work

---

1. Roughly speaking, till about 9 A.M.
2. *Tertia* = *the third* in Latin; the third hour is the mid-point between sunrise and noon.

assigned them until None. At the first signal for the Hour of None let everyone break off from his work and hold himself ready for the sounding of the second signal. After the meal let them apply themselves to their reading or to the psalms. (*Rule* 48)

Therefore, from October 1 until the six-and-a-half weeks of Lent, Benedict did not take a meal until three in the afternoon, which we would find very ascetic, if we had been active since at least an hour before sunrise; it may not have been so different from the custom of his contemporaries as from ours. As we will see, the Lenten meal was taken almost two hours later.

On the days of Lent, from morning until the end of the third hour let them apply themselves to their reading, and from then until the end of the tenth hour let them do the work assigned them. And in these days of Lent they shall each receive a book from the library, which they shall read straight through from the beginning. (*Rule* 48)

Benedictines still take this instruction literally; it is usual to choose a book suitable for Lenten reading, with the abbot's approval or at his choice. Reading something that recharges one's spiritual batteries can be highly recommended as one of the ways of "keeping Lent." The Rule also implies about three hours of reading in Lent, a little more than required in the rest of the year; and Benedict found the early hours of the morning the best time for reading, during this end-of-winter, early spring season. Others have found the same, if their work schedule permits it.

But certainly one or two of the seniors should be deputed to go about the monastery at the hours when the brethren are occupied in reading and see that there be no lazy brother who spends his time in idleness or gossip and does not apply himself to the reading, so that he is not only unprofitable to himself but also distracts others. (*Rule* 48)

In modern schools the same practice of supervising students during study periods is observed. What follows we, today, find rather surprising:

On Sundays, let all occupy themselves in reading, except those who have been appointed to various duties [e.g., work in the kitchen]. But if anyone should be so negligent and shiftless that he

will not or cannot study or read, let him be given some work to do
so that he will not be idle. (*Rule* 48)

In society at large, the observance of Sunday is, alas, somewhat neglected
today. But it is still surprising that a saint would advise work even on Sunday.
He does so, as a lesser evil than idleness, which he considers a great danger
to the soul. To someone engaged in intellectual work he might well advise
some sort of manual work, like a hobby, for Sundays: to rest the mind, without
allowing it to be idle.

Weak or sickly brethren should be assigned a task or craft of such
a nature as to keep them from idleness and at the same time not to
overburden them or drive them away with excessive toil. Their
weakness must be taken into consideration by the abbot. (*Rule* 48)

This is typical of Benedict's wisdom, warning the individual against
driving himself too hard for his own strength and the superior against cruelly
overloading his subjects.

His advice for "The Observance of Lent" is also worth recording here; it
shows how very ancient the practice of keeping Lent is, and it is still good
advice, that it be kept *joyfully* (cf. what our Lord says in Mt 6:16 about
fasting) but with *humility*, that is, without a show of excessive asceticism:

Although the life of a monk ought to have about it at all times
the character of a Lenten observance, yet since few have the strength
for that, we therefore urge that during the actual days of Lent the
brethren keep their lives most pure and at the same time wash away
during these holy days all the negligences of other times. [Work at
breaking some bad habit.] And this will be worthily done if we
restrain ourselves from all vices and give ourselves up to prayer with
tears, to reading, to compunction of heart and to abstinence. During
these days, therefore, let us increase somewhat the usual burden of
our service, as by private prayers and by abstinence in food and
drink. Thus everyone of his own will may offer God "with joy of
the Holy Spirit" something above the measure required of him.
From his body, that is, he may withhold some food, drink, sleep,
talking and jesting; and with the joy of spiritual desire he may look
forward to holy Easter. Let each one, however, suggest to his abbot
what it is that he wants to offer, and let it be done with his blessing

and approval. For anything done without the permission of the spiritual father will be imputed to presumption and vainglory and will merit no reward. (*Rule* 49)

There should be a balance of both Mary and Martha in Benedictine life (cf. Lk 10:38-41), so there is one type of manual labor which Benedict required everyone to do, as an act of charity toward the brethren; these words have bearing on the spiritual values to be found in family life:

> Let the brethren serve one another, and let none be excused from the kitchen service except by reason of sickness or occupation in some important work, for this service brings increase of reward and of charity. (*Rule* 35)

Having added that in some circumstances weaker brethren will need extra help in doing this and specified who should be excused from it entirely, he adds:

> Let the rest serve one another in charity. . . . An hour before the meal let the weekly servers each receive a drink and some bread over and above the appointed allowance, in order that at the meal time they may serve their brethren without murmuring and without excessive fatigue. On solemn days, however, let them wait until after Mass. (*Rule* 35)

Once again, we have an instance of Benedict's merciful spirit. We will have more to say about *murmuring*, which he considers one of the worst things in a community. It also appears that Mass was only celebrated on Sundays and feast days, as is still the custom in the Eastern Christian Churches.

The value he placed both on silence and on reading appears in chapter 38:

> The meals of the brethren should not be without reading. There should be a reader for the whole week, entering that office on Sunday. . . . Brothers will read and sing, not according to rank, but according to their ability to benefit their hearers.

Not everyone can read to others in a way that is clearly understood (or sing well in choir); people might take pride in the ability to do it, so they need prayers. Benedict does not want idle chatter at table but neither does he want his monks' minds to wander or be too engrossed in food, hence the recommendation of reading to them. (While the servers "live Martha" during the meal, the reader helps the others to "live Mary.")

Punishment for Faults

Benedict valued community life so highly, that what he thought of as the greatest punishment for faults against its observance was "excommunication," that is, requiring a person to be alone:

> Let the brother who is guilty of a weightier fault be excluded both from the table and from the oratory. Let none of the brethren join him either for company or for conversation. Let him be alone at the work assigned him, abiding in penitential sorrow and pondering that terrible sentence of the apostle where he says that a man of that kind is handed over for the destruction of the flesh, that the spirit may be saved in the day of the Lord. Let him take his meals alone in the measure and at the hour which the abbot shall consider suitable for him. (*Rule* 25)

For Benedict, to be cut off from the company and conversation of people, especially of one's own religious family, is a terrible punishment; it is to be cut off from the joy of Christ's presence among his disciples and to be cut off from him whom we serve and receive in many ways mentioned above.

Alas, in these misanthropic times of little faith, human company is not seen that way, and to be left alone, not required or even allowed to come to church, might feel to some more like a privilege than a punishment. However, those who think they desire solitude would find that long periods of it breed loneliness and depression. As we saw in our chapter about the abbot, Benedict would not allow the excommunicated to be neglected and left alone entirely; the abbot himself or his *senpectae* would show them great solicitude and try to bring them back into fraternal unity. So if we belong to a community, or have a family, Benedict would tell us to appreciate its members. It may be as it is with health, which we appreciate as a great gift only when we lose it.

Short of outright expulsion from the monastery—for such faults as we saw in the chapter on the Prologue (pp. 55-56), and in considering the case of a prior under the "fourth degree of humility" (p. 71)—excommunication, as we have described it, was the severest punishment Benedict prescribed, with the proviso, however, "that the brother understands the seriousness of that penalty; if he is perverse, however, let him undergo corporal punishment." (Benedict would consider us "perverse" if we thought of excommunication as a privilege rather than a punishment!) Corporal punishment is

foreign to our ideas of human dignity, but it is possible that Benedict's
contemporaries thought of it as we think of shock treatment, sometimes
effective in curing behavior resulting from attitudes of mind unacceptable
both to society and to the patient himself, such as severe depression.

For a clue as to what Benedict included under "weightier faults," we must
turn to chapter 23, "On Excommunication for Faults":

> If a brother is found to be obstinate, or disobedient, or proud, or
> murmuring, or habitually transgressing the Holy Rule in any point
> and contemptuous of the orders of his seniors, the latter shall
> admonish him secretly a first and a second time, as our Lord
> commands. If he fails to amend, let him be given a public rebuke in
> front of the whole community. But if even then he does not reform,
> let him be placed under excommunication, provided that he under-
> stands the seriousness of that penalty.

These are all faults against unity and humility. Benedict nowhere men-
tions faults against sexual morality; we cannot help wondering why, since
(in these latter decades of the twentieth century) we hear so much about acts
of homosexuality and pedophilia, committed even by clergy. It is hard to
believe Benedict never thought of that as a possibility in his monastery. There
is a phrase or two in the Rule which could be interpreted as a precaution or
warning against this kind of human weakness:

> Let them take their rest by tens or twenties with the seniors who
> have charge of them. A lamp is to be kept burning in the room . . .
> the younger brethren shall not have beds next to one another.
> (*Rule* 22)

But these precautions are more likely to be for the preservation of silence.
In the chapter "On Good Zeal" we read: "Let them tender the charity of
brotherhood chastely" (*Rule* 72). (Why add "chastely" unless it might be
tendered another way?) To the frankly curious as to what Benedict advised
about this possibility, one must answer that he says nothing explicitly about
it at all. But anyone who reads the entire Rule will see that Benedict allows
the monks no privacy, which virtually removes the possibility of this problem
arising (or other problems, such as theft from private property).

We can only speculate as to why he makes no mention of it, despite being
such a realist. Probably he would prefer monks not to think about it, a good

pastoral method of keeping the desire, suspicion, or fear of it out of their minds. We must not imagine that every society was as aware of it as our own. An American told the present writer he did not know such a vice existed until after he had graduated from college (in the first decade of this century), a college somewhat notorious for the natural vices. That does not mean homosexuality is something new, only that if it happened it was well concealed. He would have known of its possibility, if he had read his Bible as carefully as Benedict did.

We may wonder what Benedict would have done about homosexual misconduct, if it occurred. There is no evidence that he would expel a monk guilty of a lapse of this kind but repentant. (In this he differs from Don Bosco, the nineteenth century founder of the Salesian Order). There is no way of knowing for certain, but it seems more likely that he would have treated it as any other "weightier fault," with isolation "in penitential sorrow" from the company of the brethren but with great solicitude on the abbot's part, who must

> not shut his eyes to the faults of offenders; but . . . cut out those faults by the roots as soon as they appear, trying every remedy for their unhealthy behavior . . . knowing that what he has undertaken is the care of weak souls and not a tyranny over strong ones. He must console the wavering brother, comforting him that he may not be overwhelmed by excessive grief, but that charity may be strengthened in him. Let everyone pray for him. (*Rule* 2 and 28)

A hint that this was, or would have been, Benedict's policy, lies in his reference to Paul (in 1 Cor 5) having passed "that terrible sentence" [of excommunication] on "a man of that kind," that is, a man guilty of incest (living with his father's wife).

Instead of punishing the crime after it is committed, Benedict does what he can to prevent it from happening, anticipating *Perfectae Caritatis*: "Above all, everyone should remember—superiors especially—that chastity has stronger safeguards in a community when true fraternal love thrives among its members." And: "They should take advantage of those natural helps which favor mental and bodily health" (#12). The same Vatican decree advises that "Candidates should not undertake the profession of chastity . . . except . . . if they have the needed degree of psychological and emotional maturity." What was quoted above (pp. 44 and 130) about the discernment

of spirits, in the probation of candidates for the brotherhood, implies discernment of that kind of emotional stability and maturity.

Communication and Consultation

This is another necessary aspect of community life. (Were it not for this
chapter "On Calling the Brethren for Counsel," which immediately follows
the chapter on the abbot, one might think Benedict's ideal for the abbot was
too autocratic.)

> Whenever any important business has to be done in the monas-
> tery, let the abbot call together the whole community and state the
> matter to be acted upon. Then, having heard the brethren's advice,
> let him turn the matter over in his own mind and do what he shall
> judge to be most expedient. The reason we have said that all should
> be called for counsel is that the Lord often reveals to the younger
> what is best. (*Rule* 3)

As if echoing Benedict, *Perfectae Caritatis* says: "All members of the
community have a share in the welfare of the whole community and a
responsibility for it. In decisions which involve the future of an institute as
a whole, superiors should in an appropriate manner consult the members and
give them a hearing" (#4 and #14).

> Let the brethren give their advice with all the deference required
> by humility and not presume stubbornly to defend their opinions;
> but let the decision rather depend on the abbot's judgment and all
> submit to whatever he shall decide for their welfare. However, just
> as it is proper for the disciples to obey their master, so also it is his
> function to dispose all things with prudence and justice.
> In all things, therefore, let all follow the Rule as guide, and let no
> one be so rash as to deviate from it. Let no one in the monastery
> follow his heart's fancy; and let no one presume to contend with his
> abbot in an insolent way or even outside of the monastery. . . . At
> the same time, the abbot himself should do all things in the fear of
> God and in observance of the Rule. . . . But if the business to be
> done in the interests of the monastery be of lesser importance, let
> him take counsel with the seniors only. It is written, "Do everything

with counsel, and you will not repent when you have done it."
(*Rule* 3)

This advice "to do everything with counsel" is good for any individual making decisions but especially for administrators. On the one hand, the top executive must take the final responsibility (as the saying goes, "the buck stops here"). But the abbot is not an absolute ruler; he is bound to abide by the Rule as a constitutional monarch or president is bound by his country's laws and constitution, or the president of a company by its bylaws. Its members then know what are their rights and feel a shared responsibility for the community's spiritual and temporal welfare. It is always wise for an administrator to let his colleagues or employees know that his door and his ears are open. Cuthbert Butler, a famous abbot early in this century, always left his door open in the day hours and said that there are two persons in a monastery that have to sacrifice their "peace": the abbot and the Cellarer.

Epilogue

If Saint Benedict's rule of life seems to you the opposite of the typical attitude today (and therefore rather hard to put into practice: it means swimming against the current), then you have certainly understood it, and you have hopefully found the key to at least some of the problems troubling the world. The majority of us are aware that something is profoundly wrong; Benedict is confident that if we would but follow his principles, it could be put right.

Marxism has not succeeded. What goes by the name of "freedom" is in trouble. Is it really freedom anyway? Some Americans say they feel enslaved to the dollar. Perhaps; but are not too many seeking *absolute* freedom for every individual, which leads to chaos and to the slavery Christ referred to when he said: "Everyone who lives in sin is the slave of sin" (for instance, of pride)? But, "If you live according to my teaching, then you will know the truth, and the truth will set you free" (Jn 8:31, 32, 34). Human freedom is freedom under the law of God, of nature, and of civilized society, which implies some limitation to personal freedom in the name of "order" and "harmony," and the need for symbiosis with others.[1] Benedict has a strong sense of order.

A superficial reading of Benedict's ideal of obedience might see it as a renunciation of freedom. Freedom is the ability to do what you love, love understood as a free choice, and Benedict's obedience is "the virtue of those who hold nothing dearer to them," love nothing more, "than Christ." It is a human way of participating in the life of the Blessed Trinity, the Father's whole life being poured out in love for his only-begotten Son; this love is the Spirit of his life, lived in absolute freedom. He is the only being for whom absolute freedom is possible. For us a great measure of freedom is possible; it is something to which we have a right and for which we have a need; but it is limited, since it does not include a right to be selfish, which would be a contradiction of love. It is a gift we use too often in a negative way, to abuse

---

1. Cf. John D. Zizioulas, *Being As Communion* (Crestwood: Saint Vladimir's Seminary Press, 1985), p. 43.

ourselves or others. Freedom used in a positive way is the perfect fulfillment of the person.

Honorare omnes homines (to respect all human beings) is the first of the Instruments of Good Works which follow those taken from the Ten Commandments; it puts limits on the way we should treat our neighbor. Benedict wishes us to show hospitality especially to those who are "of the household of the faith" (cf. Gal 6:10) but not *only* to them. And that goes for all appropriate expressions of love and respect, that is, to the opposite sex, to young and old, and to people who have committed crimes or have failed in other ways. In word or deed we may be able to lend them our support, not in a proud condescending way but *honoring* and humbly respecting them. It begins in the way we *think* of them; then we will "not do to another what one would not have done to oneself" (*Rule* 4, #9), abusing our freedom in their regard.

An aspect of this respect for others, and for ourselves, is #24 among the Instruments of Good Works: *Veritatem ex corde et ore proferre* (to utter truth from heart and mouth). A Benedictine who is now a cardinal in Rome was quoted (when he was much younger) as saying that of all the maxims in chapter 4 of the Rule, this is the most difficult to practice. There are times when it is not appropriate to say exactly what you feel. All the same, Benedict evidently was aware how basic this is to emotional health in human relationships and implicitly also as a guideline for personal prayer: to honestly and courageously speak one's mind. How we appreciate others who are always their true selves, who can be trusted to "tell it like it is," even though the truth hurts them or us at the moment! There are inappropriate ways of doing it, to be avoided, but they are more easily forgiven than hypocrisy, secretiveness, and all forms of deception. How can others know us, understand us, help us, like or dislike us, unless we tell them what we know or what we really feel inside? John Powell, S.J., has written a best-seller about this: *Why Am I Afraid to Tell You Who I Am?* We are afraid of the truth, too much concerned with "image," and yet the truth is really so much more loveable than an image. Politicians, lawyers, and salesmen are criticized for telling half-truths (or downright lies) in order to manipulate us. But who does not do the same?

"Keep your tongue from evil and your lips that they speak no guile" (Ps 34:14) was quoted in the Prologue and: "Let us listen to the Lord as he shows us the way to that tent: 'He who speaks truth from his heart; who has not used his tongue for deceit' " (Ps 15:2-3). There are many aspects of honesty and sincerity: toward others in speech and in keeping one's word, and also within one's heart, honesty with ourselves, which takes courage. The soul owes it to itself to be clear about its own feelings, its fundamental purpose and standards: What exactly am I after? How do I expect to get there? Do I need to change? Once that is firmly settled, all that is left is to direct all we do consistently with that purpose.

We should not fail to mention a limit Benedict puts, at least a dozen times, on free speech; we meet this in his frequent condemnation of murmuring or grumbling, which in chapter 23 he even gives as just cause for excommunication. (One who has served on submarines in the Navy knows how only one person can disturb the peace and risk making everybody on the ship, or in a community, miserable.) In chapter 41, "At What Hours the Meals Should Be Taken," he acknowledges that there can be cause for grumbling (food is often the occasion for it):

> The abbot should adapt and arrange everything in such a way that souls may be saved and that the brethren may do their work without just cause for murmuring. (*Rule* 41)

But if there is just cause, the appropriate person for the monk to tell his complaints is "the person over him" and the appropriate manner is "in a quiet way and at an opportune time, without pride, resistance, or contradiction," as we saw above in our chapter on God. There is no need to repeat here what is on pp. 118-19 above about the loving way in which obedience should be given (through superiors) to God, essentially the same being quoted in our chapter on the Prologue (pp. 54-55). "Above all, let not the evil of murmuring appear for any reason whatsoever in the least word or sign. If anyone is caught at it, let him be placed under very severe discipline," wrote Benedict in chapter 34 (after insisting that the abbot see to it that everyone has what he needs). He said the same in the chapter "On the Measure of Drink":

> But where the circumstances of the place are such that not even the measure [of wine] prescribed above can be supplied, but much less or none at all, let those who live there bless God and not murmur. Above all things do we give this admonition, that they abstain from murmuring. (*Rule* 40)

"Idle talk provides an occasion for the evil one," says chapter 43 of the Rule; so "those who come late to the Work of God" should not be required "to remain outside of the oratory." Benedict's intention is that the house of God should be a peaceful scene, but even in the Garden of Eden there was a snake in the grass, a fly in the ointment, the devil. Like all the early Christians, Benedict did not believe the devil described in the Bible was only a metaphorical symbol of evil; he had met him personally, as we saw in chapter 1.

> [Gifts received] from a monk's parents, or anyone else, or from his brethren, should be shown to the abbot; but [if the abbot does not allow it to be received], the brother to whom it was sent should not be grieved, *lest occasion be given to the devil.* (*Rule* 54)

Other voices can be heard within us besides that of the Holy Spirit: in chapter 58, "a monk who decides to leave the monastery (which God forbid)" is said to "listen to the persuasions of the devil." In the Prologue Benedict quoted the psalm which asks, " 'Who will dwell in the tent of [God's] kingdom, or rest on his holy mountain?' He who, under any temptation from the malicious devil, has brought him to naught by casting him and his temptation from the sight of his heart; and who has laid hold of his thoughts while they were still young and dashed them against Christ." Christ is a real presence to Benedict, so is the devil. Were one to write an adaptation of C. S. Lewis' *Screwtape Letters,* or a theatrical play to dramatize the spiritual life of a monk, the devil would have to be included in the cast. Chapter 1 of the Rule describes monastic life as "a fight against the devil" (mostly within the thoughts of one's mind, as we have seen); and priors "inflated with the evil spirit of pride [who] consider themselves second abbots [and] give rise to grave scandals by usurping power and causing dissensions" are among those who get worsted in the contest. Pride, murmuring, grief, departure, any temptation succumbed to, are all points scored by the devil. Humility, joyful obedience, and perseverance are points scored by the monk (or by Christ within him).

In opposition to the spirit of selfishness and pride, the Benedictine spirit is one of humility, a commitment to follow him who said frequently in the gospels: "He who exalts himself will be humbled, and who humbles himself will be exalted"—exalted one hopes to the perfection of the love of God and neighbor. Who has arrived at that, has nothing more to worry about or to fear. The monk enters into the mystery of the humility of Christ himself, who led the way through the renunciation of divine riches to the humiliation of being obedient even to death on a cross, rewarded by being raised to the right hand of the Father (cf. Phil 2:3-9, and the Nicene Creed). This ideal was already that of the Egyptian monks of whom Benedict read in Cassian, from whom he was willing to learn and make their ideal his own, his talent being the ability to present it in a concise practical rule of life for a community.

Wise psychologists warn us that the pursuit of humility and acceptance of the renunciation of one's own will can be depressing. But a vital faith in the mystery of Christ can transform it into something exalting, elating, and optimistic. It must be motivated by love, usually as a goal to be reached, motivating the beginnings only imperfectly, that is, with an admixture of the fear of God and of his just punishments. Whereas spiritual writers today urge us to love, the ancients stressed humility at the start; so long as we do not have the wrong idea of humility as something depressing and demeaning, this can still today be very practical for those of us whose idea of love is somewhat distorted in comparison with what it means in the gospels. Christ's humility and obedience was not lived without dignity and was the supreme expression, in his humanity, of his love for his Father.

It may be easier to delude oneself about having the virtue of charity and love than about humility. But here too one can be deluded; there can be "illusions of humility" as well as "illusions of grandeur." Sentimentality is not identical with the love of God, nor is self-abasement and self-hate identical with Christ's humility. Let us pray to know the truth about ourselves, to be free of illusions, trusting in the help and enlightenment of grace, and "never despair of the mercy of God" (*Rule* 4, #72).

Saint Gregory told us (cf. p. 25) that Benedict possessed the Spirit of only one Person, Christ the Savior. Jesus' doctrine recorded in the New Testament had been directed to disciples who were a tiny minority (a "little flock" "surrounded by wolves," cf. Lk 10:3; 12:32); his teaching was not destined to form the basis for the organization of a public institution until later on. After five centuries had passed, the Empire was no longer officially hostile, it had even adopted Christianity as the state religion. But its structures had collapsed in the West, its power was severely weakened. One might almost say that out there in central Italy Benedict "died to himself" at roughly the age of eighteen and was taken over by the soul of Christ, who wrote the Rule as a practical application of his gospel to a Christian society or community in a world that could be trusted to tolerate it. Men and women adopted it as their rule of life, not to glorify themselves (the vast majority remain nameless in history), but to glorify God through the peace their communities would spread through war-torn Europe and eventually beyond, saving thereby much of the legacy of Roman civilization as well as bringing or preserving the presence of Christ. The Rule then is a gift of Christ's Spirit to the world. To ignore it without opening it might make God feel something like you would feel if you sent your child, or a friend, a present at Christmas, something you had gone to some trouble to choose for them, only to discover months or even years later that, though received, the package had never been opened.[1] Benedict permitted himself an equally anthropomorphic metaphor about God's imagined "feelings," in the Prologue: "Beg of him with most earnest prayer . . . that he who has now deigned to count us among his sons may not at any time *be grieved by our evil deeds*. For we must always so serve him with the good things he has given us, that he will never as an angry Father disinherit his children."

---

1. Christopher Derrick's, *The Rule of Peace, Saint Benedict and the European Future* (Petersham: Saint Bede's Publications, 1980) enlarges on the theme of the practical application of Saint Benedict's Rule, as the title implies; the author adds in the Preface that his book is relevant to all continents which share in the inheritance of Europe.

Acknowledgments

Excerpts from *Life and Miracles of St. Benedict* and *St. Benedict's Rule for Monasteries* (©1948 by The Order of St. Benedict, Inc., published by The Liturgical Press, Collegeville, Minnesota) are used with permission from the publisher.

Thanks to Brother Francis Crowley for reading the manuscript and making many helpful suggestions, and to Mrs. Donald Culver for her help.